The Joy of Letting Go

The Joy of Letting Go

Helpful thoughts for Challenging Times

SUZANNE FALTER

The Joy of Letting Go
Copyright © 2019 by Suzanne Falter, LLC

Published by
Love and Happiness Publishing
Oakland, CA

Designed by Danielle H. Acee, The Authors' Assistant
Cover by Dissect Designs

All rights reserved. This book may not be reproduced in whole or in part, without written permission from the publisher, except by a reviewer who may quote brief passages in a review; nor may any part of this book be reproduced, stored in a retrieval system, or transmitted in any form or by any means electronic, mechanical, photocopying, recording, or other, without written permission from the publisher.

ISBN: 978-0-9911248-4-8

Printed in the United States of America

*For Luke
with love*

Contents

Introduction 1

Eight Important Lessons I Learned When I Lost Everything 5

Is Letting Go the Key to Happiness? (Absolutely!) 9

The Magic and the Challenge of Letting Go 13

What Wildfires Can Teach Us About Letting Go 17

How to Keep the Faith When All Hell is Breaking Loose 20

Are You on a Hero's Journey? 23

How to Stop Being a Victim and Love Life Again 28

Getting Through the Pain of a Transition 32

What's Really Going on When Women Cry for 'No Reason' 35

Should You Quit Pursuing Your Dreams or Hang In There? 38

The Secret to Relaxing About Life 41

In Praise of Reality and Why We Hide from It 44

How to Stop Doing So Much and Start Receiving More 47

The Eight Secrets of Emotional Self-Care 50

Getting Out of the Cage of Self-Doubt 53

The Five-Minute Antidote To Your Fear 56

How to Move on When the Time is Right 59

How to Walk Away from 'Should' 62

Discovering That I Am Worth It 65

How a Career Full of Failures Taught Me About Real Success 69

How I Learned to Stop Fighting and Heal My Anger 73

The Thirty-Minute Exercise That Helped Me Forgive and Forget 76

How to Give Yourself the Pep Talk You Deserve 79

How to Find the Lessons Hidden in Everyday Dilemmas 82

How to Be Alone, Even on Your Birthday 84

How to Stop Trying to Get Meditation Right and Just Relax 87

What's on the Other Side of Letting Go? It's Flow, Baby! 90

Tapping into the Joy of Life 93

How to Take a Day Off So It Really Counts 97

The Value of a 'Why Not?' List 101

How I Gave Up My Home and Found Freedom 104

Seven Simple Ideas for a Happier Life 108

How I Finally Learned to Open My Heart 110

A Lesson in Being from Teal 114

A Very Brief Introduction

This book was created for every person in the world who ever felt stuck, frustrated, confused, afraid, lonely, or grief. Perhaps you find yourself at a crossroads—a place where you must confront a grim reality in order to move forward. Yet, if you stay, you know you will suffer unduly.

Maybe you have to say goodbye to a beloved person, place, or pet. Or maybe you've got to let go of a job, a career, a habit or an experience that's no longer a good fit in your life. Or maybe what you're letting go of is simply an outgrown way of thinking or being.

Perhaps you're grieving something that was taken away from you, seemingly by brute force.

All you know is that the going is rough, and you want this to be over as soon as possible. You don't like the pain, and you really don't like all that lurking uncertainty.

My friend, whatever your challenge is, you will get through this. Once you finally give up the struggle, the resistance and the fear, and just surrender, then you are set free. That's when letting go becomes a remarkably simple affair.

Surprisingly, letting go is the magic key that unlocks the door of your full potential. It is the soothing tonic that gives you unexpected clarity and wisdom. It's the passport to opportunities you never would have expected. For once you let go, you give the Universe a very clear message: that you are ready for the next thing to arrive.

But first you truly must surrender—no matter how scared you are. For this is the way of the world.

In the year or two before my daughter Teal died, she believed she'd been put on this earth to be a healer. She willingly abandoned a budding music career as a blues singer in Austin, Texas, and moved to San Francisco to find her 'healing gift' as she put it. She thought it had something to do with helping women manage their panic and anxiety, so she created an eclectic program of study at the local college.

"Something really big is going to happen that will give me my healing gift," Teal told me over dinner one night, several months before her death. She was going to do this thing, come hell or high water. She wasn't a bit concerned about giving up the singing she'd just spent two years studying at Berklee College of Music. Nor was she worried about moving three thousand miles to a city where she knew no one except me. And I was newly arrived myself.

Instead, she let go of it all and simply showed up with a few hundred dollars in the bank. Then she followed her guidance and her heart from one stepping stone to the next…until her death nine months later from a medically unexplainable cardiac arrest.

At the time, Teal kept a tattered red spiral notebook filled with insights she received in her daily meditations. I held this notebook close to me in the years following her death, absorbing the simple wisdom on every page. And so, Teal became a healer…my healer. May she will become yours, as well.

Teal summarized the situation well when it comes to letting go, when she wrote this:
> *Fear is just another way of saying no.*
> *Practice yes in all areas of your life to learn to let it go.*

These essays are not arranged in exact chronological order, but rather in an order of the heart. Each one tracks my path toward just a little more letting go, and the happy results I discovered on the other side.

You might want to read them from start to finish. Or you might want to open the book to a random page when you need a bit of encouragement. Either way, let the book, itself, tell you how to explore letting go.

May it guide you and comfort you well. And may you truly discover the innate joy that blossoms when you do finally let go.

Eight Important Lessons I Learned When I Lost Everything

Was there ever a time in your life when you lost something very precious to you…and became better for it?

This was very much on my mind some years back, as I healed from losing everything—relationship, marriage, home, career, my daughter and then my mother.

What I came to realize is that this total meltdown was an extremely powerful and necessary experience. I would even say my soul demanded it, for that is how it is with crisis and loss. They teach you how to let go, for once and for all.

A breakdown happens because something in our system requires it in order to move ahead. The status quo cannot go on. We are being called upon—even forced—to grow.

When all of this came down in my own life, I was lost. I was living in a sketchy apartment building in which the super was a prowler who actually invaded apartments when the tenants were out. The flu I'd had for six months made no sign of stopping, and I was struggling to keep my head above water in a toxic relationship that degraded me a little more every day. I was working constantly, doing everything I could to avoid the fact that my partner was not in love with me, and that I was profoundly miserable.

Meanwhile, the business I'd come to California to begin took off, exploded, and then promptly burned out. Yet instead of stopping to regroup, I blindly dove into yet another business partnership I didn't need or even want. Or even fully understand.

None of it felt right. And yet all of it, magically, was very right, because each of these experiences taught me something critical to my growth.

It wasn't until everything began to unravel that things started to feel better—even though the circumstances were heinous. I walked willingly into that void of nothingness, mainly because I had no other choice.

Even in my grief, I could see the integrity of what was happening. Here are some of the realizations that landed then…and still resound every day in my life.

1. **You don't have to heal alone.** Whether you realize this or not, you have many supportive circles of friends around you. I thought I had few friends when my own breakdown began, but somehow they just started showing up, and my network expanded as I became more comfortable asking for help. Supportive friends make the ride so much easier. In fact, they are critical.

2. **It's OK to be in the Void for a while.** The Void, while scary at first, is an enormously creative place. If you can tolerate the stillness and the uncertainty, eventually life returns when you are ready. Ideas drop in. Joy descends. Feel free to stretch out and hang here for a while. It's actually a great place to heal.

3. **You don't have to know the answers right now.** Or ever, really. You just have to know what you know right now. And know that this is enough and you will, indeed, be fine.

4. **Grace happens when you least expect it.** Again and again, I have been surprised by the incredible generosity of others,

which always magically arrives at just the right moment—in ways I couldn't even plan or hope for. This grace seems to be linked to being in the flow, the enjoyment of life. When I'm not focusing on it, the solution or the desired outcome always seem to arrive. Reminder: the Universe wants us to be happy. So why not go with the flow?

5. **We won't get 'there' by striving** (wherever 'there' is.) Instead, what if life was like a great takeout delivery service? You decide you want Chinese, you make a call, then sit down to watch TV. Suddenly, at just the perfect moment, the doorbell rings and in comes steaming Moo Shu Pork. While having goals and ideas is commendable, pushing doesn't work. Making the request and allowing it to be delivered by the great power of the Universe does. And yeah, you do have to show up and get some things done, of course. And the Universe will only deliver in its own good time. But striving and pushing truly is optional.

6. **You are whole and perfect just as you are.** Yeah, we all have rough edges. Every day I say a prayer asking that my character defects be removed. Meanwhile, this fairly messy package is what I've got to work with, so I try to accept my various scars and wounds that make life hard sometimes. As long as you do your best to do no harm, and to show up honestly and in good faith, the rest truly will be taken care of. Don't forget your innate perfection…it's a key to letting go.

7. **You have everything you need right now.** It may not look like it, but I'm here to vouch for this fact. My own breakdown meant two years of living extremely simply, which became an unexpected delight. I found low cost gems like

consignment clothing, an old-fashioned flip phone and camping. And even living in the guest room of a dear friend. During these precious months, I found I was liberated. I no longer did work 'just for the money,' and began to tune in to the true pleasures in life. Then, when I started to need income, employment smoothly showed up right on time. For this is the flow of life. If you can push past your fear, you will see you do, indeed, have enough right here and right now.

8. **Freedom is the point.** Janis Joplin wails that freedom is just another word for nothing left to lose. But personally, I felt richer than I ever could have imagined during my breakdown. While I didn't have much by some standards, i.e. no house, no mortgage, or even a family member nearby, I truly appreciated my life and was able to wake up each day feeling taken care of and fulfilled…even when I was grieving.

So yeah, there's an end to the rainbow if you follow it. And ironically it's about seizing what is here and now. That's my invitation to you in this moment, this hour, this day, my dear friend.

And do remember, you truly are not alone.

Is Letting Go the Key to Happiness? (Absolutely!)

Question: what do you long for?

What, in your heart of hearts, do you know you could have if only…

If only, what? You won the lottery? You had more time because you didn't have this [insert person, place or thing] that holds you back?

If so, then it could be time to surrender—but only if you are willing to let go. (And I do mean completely.)

Here's the catch.

Innate to the human condition is a certain level of suffering that is just…there. We somehow have it wired up that we must suffer on some level. It's just part of being human, right? Perhaps people were not kind to us when we were young, so we think we deserve a certain amount of pain. Or perhaps we made a karmic decision before we entered this life that we would have all sorts of lessons, usually delivered through harshness.

Whatever the case may be, we are mere babes as we move through this life and subject ourselves to a huge amount of suffering. Yes, we think we are all powerful, wielding credit cards, cell phones, tight schedules and big demands. Yet, behind all of that posturing is our fear.

We are afraid that our suffering will catch up with us. That we will lose our steely grip on control and be brought to our knees by circumstance. Or that we will lose everything, and so we will crumble to the ground and die.

What we don't see is that when we have nothing, when we finally let go and fall apart, then we finally become free.

In that moment, we become surrendered enough to acknowledge the truth—that all of this resistance and suffering we've cooked up is unnecessary. We start to see that we can have anything we want, but only if we will allow ourselves to trust the Universe to bring it our way. We start to get it that we can't push a river—nor can we force the flow of life.

Ranier Maria Rilke wrote: "Will is of little importance, complaining is nothing, fame is nothing. Openness, patience, receptivity, solitude is everything."

If we can allow ourselves to relax into that receptivity and stop the incessant striving and pushing, then the river can finally, truly turn our way. Perhaps for you that critical surrender means losing a treasured client or contract you'd wanted forever.

Without that guaranteed source of income you think you will never make it. You believe you will simply dissolve, and cease to be the glorious You that you keep trying to be.

Ah, but friend, what if …

What if the real You is actually waiting behind all the letting go and the chaos? What if the Universe has something even better prepared for you that you can't even imagine? Can you let go and surrender into that infinite possibility?

This is when your heart opens, your love for the world expands and you are finally set free.

When I gave up my twenty-five-year marriage, my big showcase home, and my identity as a nice straight lady, I began to surrender and truly fall apart. I moved across the country, came out as a lesbian and started all over again. For a while everything seemed rosy. But then suddenly, it all got very dark indeed.

Within two years I'd closed my business, lost my relationship and the home that came with it. For a while I roamed around, staying with friends here and there, not sure exactly what to do. Then, incredibly, my daughter died. Six months later to the day, my mother died as well.

So the bottom dropped out completely.

Yet this was not the end. Rather, it was a powerful beginning. The lessons that followed were intense and immediate. Since then my life has come full circle into an amazing alignment in which every day I feel more confident, more powerful and stronger than ever before.

And all I had to do was let go. Completely.

There is something unexpected and sweet about the state of non-attachment that follows. The usual supports are gone. Within that ultimate moment of self-reliance, devoid of all your usual props, you finally discover what you are truly made of. And what you are made of is love.

You are not your judgments, your hurts or your long list of to-do's. Nor are you your self-criticisms and your relentless drive for perfection. Yet, within that swirl of chaos, you discover you are loved and supported in ways you'd never imagined.

No, dear friend, in the end you are nothing more than your big, beating heart. The degree to which you can know and live this love is the degree to which you honor the path you have been given.

There is no valor in holding back in the name of practicality. Do that thing you have been given to do in the small of your heart—the one that propels you forward with an 'if only…' That is where the magic is.

If it means some carefully constructed structures must dissolve as you face your worst fears, then so be it. On the other side of all that loss is freedom.

You will survive. In fact, you will probably thrive; I can promise you that. That dream of yours is like a great beam of love waiting to pour out into the world and light your path as it lights others. Within that divine consciousness is all the magic and power in the world.

Why resist, dear friend? Why not just dissolve? For I can tell you this right now with a smile and an arm around your shoulders. Not only do you deserve it…we all do.

We truly do long for your gifts.

So will you just surrender?

The Magic and the Challenge of Letting Go

When confronted with a massive life transition, I will hang on like a terrier, sinking my sharp little teeth in deeper and deeper, until simple exhaustion finally forces me to let go.

I'm happy to say the terrier lets go far more easily these days. But only because I've learned what lies on the other side of that monumental letting go.

What do I mean by 'letting go?'

Letting go is recognizing that:
1. Something doesn't work
2. Something will not change on its own accord
3. A fundamental truth needs to be told…followed by action

In other words, I must step out of denial and back into reality.

A relationship I had comes to mind. It was a classic case of the rabid terrier refusing to own the truth that there was no way the two of us were going to 'make it.' All we were making was a mess, which we'd been making since day one.

I was in denial about the following things:
- My would-be partner was not actually in love with me, although there was a great deal of 'like very much' going on.

- Her massive resistance to the relationship, including everything from frank and frequent criticism of me to withholding sex was not okay.
- It was also not okay to walk around all the time on pins and needles, trying like hell to get her to love me.
- I could not think, manage or force this relationship to be anything other than it was.

Oh, I thought I had it all figured out. But now I was endlessly clinging, endlessly strategizing and trying to change to be someone other than myself. I tried being quiet, then I tried being talkative. I tried cooking my way to redemption. Hell, I even let her pick out all of my clothing.

'*If only I could be better…then she would finally love me*' went my own diseased thinking.

What I didn't know then is that letting go always, inevitably leads to something better. It simply has to, for this is the way of the Universe. To paraphrase the movie, *The Best, Exotic Marigold Hotel*, if your problem has not yet worked out, then it is not yet the end.

Life is nothing *but* a continuous process of letting go. We are constantly being called to let go of love, money, fame, glory, acceptance, children, health, youth, and so many treasured but often unobtainable goals. It's one release after another, until finally at the end, we let go of life itself.

And always, always, on the other side of that release is the unknown. Which is exactly what we fear the most. And yet here is exactly where you find the magic.

How desperately I clung to my faux-love. I even gave up my apartment in San Francisco, bought a car, and moved into the new apartment she'd gotten in Marin County. I did this even though she came to me shortly before we moved, saying she had doubts about the relationship.

I did this even though my name was not on the lease, nor did I have a parking space. And, even though I had doubts about the relationship as well.

At the time, I was in denial, and denial is the most powerful of drugs. When she ended the relationship a few months later and I walked away, I was surprised to discover that I was relieved.

Finally, someone had the courage to tell the truth, and so the tension was lifted. The unknown had arrived. I had been thrust into the Void once again.

And, actually, the Void wasn't so bad after all. I've found it has a certain brilliance to it. For it is here that we become formless, and so we can finally, slowly embrace the truth—*our* truth. And in doing so, we transform.

This is the work of the Hindu goddess Kali, fierce lover of destruction and chaos, Goddess of Time, Change and Creation. Not long after our breakup, I put a small statue of the dancing Kali on the dashboard of my car, as I wandered, trying to find my right place.

And there she still stands, encouraging me to let go into the Void, carrying my sword and feeling my true power.

Recently I told a friend facing the Void of retirement that it's like dismantling a house. Down must go all of our dreams, our hopes and even our identity. It must all be taken apart completely, the detritus moved out and the rooms emptied. For only then can we remove the dust, sweep up the dirt and get rid of the outdated junk. Only then can true reinvention begin.

This process of letting go has its share of pain and suffering, but our inner Kali can help us to embrace it. For once the way is laid truly bare, then the sweetest transformation can take place. Then we can finally tell the truth, and begin to put the warm arm of compassion around our own shoulders.

For me, what followed the end of this relationship, and the death of my daughter three months later, was nothing less than a radical transformation of everything I was. And everything I believed.

I discovered life anew, and walked around day after day being mind blown by what I was discovering. For one thing, I found my values had been completely lost. I also realized I hadn't had much fun in forever—and that I'd set my life up to revel in addictive behaviors that did nothing for my soul.

We can walk away from such moments shaking our head, saying, "What was I thinking?" Then, slowly and with a great deal of self-care, we can begin again to rebuild, one tender step at a time. And one single day at a time.

So we become patient with ourselves, and we learn to listen to our heart as we create anew, this time informed by the wisdom of destruction.

For destruction always leads to something better. But only if we let it. There is no hurrying this process of reinvention, dear friend. Nor should there be.

There can only be surrender to the beautiful path of life, which will always deliver us just to where we need to be.

What Wildfires Can Teach Us About Letting Go

There is a huge amount of destruction going on in the world right now. Between the earthquakes, droughts, and floods, we thought we'd seen the worst of it. Then California started burning up.

In 2017, one of the biggest wildfires in California history burned out of control thirty miles to the north of my home, consuming forest, houses, roads, wineries, and pretty much everything else in its path. Once that one was contained, an even more destructive wildfire started in the next county. In 2017 alone, 47 people were killed in wildfires—more than all the wildfire deaths in the previous ten years combined.

That year more than ten thousand structures burned. This included a lovely round barn I had always admired, built in 1899. The image of it burning haunts me.

I discovered the round barn when I lived up in the wine country a few years earlier. Each week I would pick up my mail just across the highway from that barn. I was freshly grieving my daughter's death then, and trying to put my life back together in some way, shape or form. The barn reminded me of the life I'd left behind in New England, a place where there was another round barn I knew and loved. It was a place where I'd been happy.

The round barn was the last surviving structure of what was one a Utopian community at the end of the nineteenth century. Its buildings were constructed to 'ascend into the celestial sphere' once the millennium passed. But they never did.

Unless…well…maybe that's what happened in 2017. Perhaps all of these structures and homes and lives that got lost were built or born only to eventually die.

This is the part we forget in our zeal to get out there, grab life by the gonads and build our empires. All of it—even the most beloved old barn—will sooner or later be turned to dust. As will we, for this is the path of life.

Life always leads to death, for how can it not?

But consider this. What if that is the point? What if the fate of this old barn, and the other structures and lives that were lost in these fires, went down in the blaze for some larger reason? Some reason that has to do with developing gratitude, with appreciating the very fabric of life? Or perhaps with finding the lessons learned?

What if these losses led to greater kindness, compassion, love and humility and discovering the true meaning of life?

Could it be that the destruction of these wildfires and natural disasters was just life's not so gentle way of correcting us? Of putting us on course to embrace our true values and return to love?

That's what's possible when we experience extreme loss. Once we've fully and courageously embraced and processed our grief, then we can then travel to the other side of that loss and begin again.

Then we can remember all the round barns we lost, and pay tribute to them in some meaningful way that also gives back to everyone else. Our history is powerful—and when we really examine it, we are reminded how temporary life is.

One winery owner whose property was heavily damaged was able to save a letter written by his great-great grandfather who'd built the place. In the letter, he recounted the earthquake and subsequent fire that destroyed the winery back in 1906.

One hundred years later, that memento is especially significant.

In my own life, there isn't a day that goes by that I don't think of my daughter Teal. Sometimes it's in sadness, and I just wish I could hear her voice or feel her hug again. But most of the time, it's a smile at a great moment we shared, or it's the thrill of telling the story of the donation of her organs to a listening audience.

After the loss, life does and will move on again. That much we know. But first there is always the hard work of grieving to do.

May you find your own treasures in the rubble of destruction, wherever it falls in your life.

How to Keep the Faith When All Hell is Breaking Loose

For a seed to achieve its greatest expression, it must come completely undone. The shell cracks, its insides come out and everything changes. To someone who doesn't understand growth, it would look like complete destruction.

Cynthia Occelli

Do you know this place of complete surrender? Life happens and you are swept along with it. You stand in the wind and feel nothing beneath your feet as you are buffeted here and there. Yet…if you look…you will find there *is* something beneath your feet.

That something is belief, because you know it in your heart. As the wind rattles everything around you, you distantly recall platitudes about 'this too shall pass,' or something someone said about windows closing and doors opening.

But belief's a slippery bugger, and it's hard to hang in there when life seems to threaten your very existence.

Here are some things you can do to keep the faith while your own personal seed is breaking open.

1. **Remember that nothing is permanent.** Whatever is happening right now really will pass. In a year's time, it will be a memory—perhaps even sooner. And with that remembering comes perspective. Right now is possibly the worst this

experience will ever feel.

2. **You might as well embrace reality.** Trying to duck it is basically like trying to swim upstream against an impossible current. You will eventually get pushed back to that inevitable truth. So make your life easy in the end by opening that letter, making that phone call, having that conversation now. Then just let the chips fall where they may—no matter how painful. By honoring the flow of life, you will ultimately be rewarded.

3. **Enjoy what there is to be enjoyed.** There will be strange little flickers of joy (and even big ones) along the way. They are Spirit's way of saying, 'It's okay, you can take a break from all of this heaviness." I saw it all around me in that terrible week that my daughter lay dying in the hospital. At the time, I kept experiencing strange, inexplicable flashes of joy. I couldn't understand that phantom joy, but now I do. There is divinity even in great pain and loss. By recognizing it and even savoring it, you give your heart a little relief.

4. **Take time for yourself.** Whatever is challenging you, you can allow space and time to comfort yourself. You must if you are ever to get to the gold buried deep within the fire. (Did I mention there is gold there?) Take a walk, write in a journal, listen to soothing music, read something comforting. Close the door on the rest of the world and allow yourself to actively feel what you need to feel. Then breathe, and know in the end everything's going to be okay. This is where the healing happens.

5. **Ask Spirit to show you the way.** Know that this, too, is part of the divine plan, no matter how heinous or difficult your circumstance. Who said life was meant to be easy and free all the time? Where would the growth be if it was? Above all, know that God has your back, now and forever, and

nothing that happens is without reason. Whenever you need to understand more, or get more guidance, simply ask. The answer is always there.

6. **Create a bed of support.** No one says you have to cross the desert alone. It wouldn't be in your best interest to suffer excessively either. So ask for help. Call a trusted friend or five. Reach out to family. Find a good therapist. Go to a support group. Find a hospice grief group, or a hospital group for caregivers or those who are divorcing, or dealing with anxiety or depression. Try some Twelve-Step recovery groups. These are people you can learn from and support, in turn. People understand and they genuinely want to help you. They really do. These groups were probably the biggest revelation—and the greatest source of comfort—I found in my own grief recovery.

7. **Trust the process.** You may feel excruciatingly alone. You may feel like you are so lost you will never recover. But here's the thing. This is all happening for a reason, and you will never be the same again. Just allow the magic of life to do its work and set you free. Your soul will thank you for it, and you will emerge stronger and better for it. You really will.

It is only in complete surrender that you can know the most profound joy.

Believe it or not, there is magic here, friend. But you must let go to let it in.

Are You on a Hero's Journey?

Lately I've been reading about Joseph Campbell's carefully delineated 'Hero's Journey.' For those who aren't familiar with it, this is the wildly heaving ups and downs of a big adventure or a quest. It's Jesus wandering in the desert, or Harry Potter plotting against Voldemort. It's an epic trip into nothing less than your soul, and it's often what's at play when life turns us completely upside down.

Some years ago, Campbell culled the basic seventeen themes from the world of mythology to explain why we are called forth… again and again…to be tested in this mortal coil. Turns out there are big lessons here.

With my seriously abridged list below, you can make side-by-side comparisons with your own life and decide if you're on a Hero's Journey, too.

Because if you're like me, you end up on that journey whether you like it or not. The good news is that heroes are *always* delivered to a much sweeter place, and they get a lot of support along the way.

Best of all, they get to complete critical bits of their karma in this lifetime, and so grow in the process. Here's how the Hero's Journey generally unfolds.

1. **The journey begins**. A questing person (our hero) is told to make a radical change and leave behind everything she once knew to be familiar. Or perhaps circumstances take her there (an unanticipated break up, a devastating fire, a

sudden job loss). She might be feeling dead in her current life, or wildly restless or somehow dissatisfied. One way or another, the opportunity to do it all differently arrives.
2. **The hero wavers.** She might put her foot down and say, 'Hell no!' …or she might just say, 'What the hell!' and go with it.
3. **The hero gets an assistant.** Our hero decides to dive in, and suddenly a new, magical helper appears. Maybe it's a spiritual teacher, or a heavenly vision. Or maybe it's a really good astrologer. In my own case, it was a Twelve-Step sponsor, and a couple of seriously great friends.
4. **Now the hero ventures forth**, crossing into an uncertain world where there are no known rules, limits or structure. Enter uncertainty. And I do mean UNCERTAINTY. Like…about everything.
5. **Our hero goes into 'the Belly of the Beast'.** Suddenly everything is extremely unfamiliar. This marks the separation from our hero's previously known world. And there's no going back. Our hero lets go, surrenders and tells God she's ready for a transformation. (This is a very key step.) She knows she's willing to do whatever it takes to change things up.

Because basically…she has to.

6. **It's test time.** Here begins a series of challenges that come out of nowhere. The hero may fail as she goes. Or not. Will she make it?
7. **The hero experiences unconditional love.** This might be the shining knight our hero goes ape for…or it could be the loving mother that an infant yearns for at birth. Whoever it is, this source is love, pure and simple.

For me, I got in touch with that love by going to meetings with other grieving parents and recovering addicts. And by reading the journals left behind by the extraordinary love beam who was my daughter Teal. I dreamt about her, as well. Each time I did, I felt washed with love. It was incredibly healing.

8. **Temptation arrives.** What else is new? Is our hero going to keep her course steady and focused on the path toward transformation? Or is she going down the rabbit hole after distracting stuff, like Angry Birds, binging on Netflix and too many donuts? Or maybe the temptation is something bigger, like being offered the seriously wrong job for a whole lot of money.

In my case, was I going to get my compulsive financial and love issues sorted out? Or was I going to rush back to overspending, and the nearest warm bed with an appealing lover in it?

9. **Our hero confronts that one thing that has the most power in her life.** This becomes an initiation test as hero faces up to her biggest challenger. In my case it was the IRS (see below), but in many cases the entity is male, as in a father figure. And yes, my IRS appeals officer was a really sweet, fatherly guy with the power to totally break me.

The hero must prove herself again. Here is where she develops true detachment—and thus the coming to know redemption, joy and bliss.

10. **The goal of the hero's quest arrives.** This would be what Campbell called 'The Boon,' and it's that ephemeral thing the hero was after all along. So victory is sweet, at least temporarily. Though now the hero is humbled and does not see herself so much as the victorious winner but more as the keeper of a kinder, gentler, more enlightened state of being.

In the world of recovery, you might call this 'serenity'.

11. **Is our hero going to come back down to Earth?** And what about that Boon? Can she bring her transformation back

into everyday life? Can she maintain equilibrium in a traffic jam? Will she always be kind to children having tantrums? Will she do the right thing in love and money? These are the questions that Campbell's Hero's Journey leaves us with.

12. **Our hero gets help.** No one gets to do this part alone—unless they're up for a very tough time. So the hero marshals help from the Underworld or Spirit world, or maybe Task Rabbit, a good life coach or a therapist.

13. **Our hero learns to live in spiritual and material bliss**, balancing both in equal measure. At the same time our hero has really been through something, so she no longer fears death. She understands the only moment that counts is happening right now. Thus a new, truly abundant and happy life begins. One in which you're not even afraid of the IRS.

Our hero then rambles off to serve the world in great, good gratitude.

I experienced my own Hero's Journey during the two years after Teal's death. I had no idea how I'd move forward with my life, where I would ultimately live or what I'd even do. I also had no idea how I could make money. Being grief-stricken, my mojo was simply gone… until it wasn't.

In fact, I surrendered to the path. I lived in a series of guest rooms while my belongings were packed up in storage. I faced tests around setting boundaries, listening to myself, and honoring that still small voice again and again. Slowly, I learned to stop putting up with inappropriate behavior, and began saying 'No.'

I went through a radical reclaiming of myself after the IRS audited me. An MIA accountant and a newbie IRS auditor made mistakes that left me needing to appeal my errant fifty-thousand-dollar tax bill—pretty much all of the money I had at the time. I was called to prove—alone—exactly what all those mistakes were, which I did, one page at a time. Eventually I got over my fear, took the necessary steps and went through the appeals process. In the end, I walked away owing nothing.

Along the way, I also found a humbler, happier, far more authentic, life. And yep, I got help each step of the way. I also learned abundantly, and was appropriately humbled as I saw, in graphic display, how wild my overspending had been for the years in question.

Beautifully, I also found my way to a healthy and lasting love, as well. Four years after Teal's death, I married the love of my life. Now I was ready for it, because I'd done the needed homework.

I maintain these Heroes Journeys happen because we invite them in. Because we seriously need them, and so the Universe delivers, right on time.

All I know is that when you truly let go and become willing to take the journey, you will ultimately be rewarded. But you have to be willing to step into the unknown, and be reborn as someone entirely different.

The key truly is in letting go, because you can't be transformed if you're still clinging to the old, safe routine.

Joseph Campbell's Hero's Journey has a much more extensive set of stages online than I've captured here, so you might want to take a look. Just search for Hero's Journey. You'll find it.

May your own journey give you everything you truly desire. And may it teach you everything you need right now.

How to Stop Being a Victim and Love Life Again

One of the most useful discoveries I have made is that at times, I have been a great, big victim. Or rather, I was a victim—one who uses their hardships to pry sympathy and attention out of others.

I used my victimhood for years beginning as a small child, maybe only four or five years old. Then I would lie at the bottom of the stairs, hoping my distracted addict mother would come by and notice me.

"I fell down the stairs," I would whimper with a big, teary face. For a moment, she would actually stop and comfort me. This was how I learned to get love.

You know victims. We are the whiners who always seem to have some big problem at hand. We cry a lot. Or we complain, bitch and moan. The sad fact is that we know no other way to get our needs met. Yet once we can actually own our victim stance, and make a choice about it, then liberation is at hand.

I carried on as a victim for the first seven years of school, when I could be counted on to cry the moment the bullies began to taunt. It never occurred to me to stand up to them, or bully them right back, or even leave the room. Instead, I'd dissolve into a puddle of tears every single time, giving them exactly what they were looking for.

By the time I was an adult, my role as victim even got into my financial health. Time after time, I'd dissolve into tears at the accountants' office when I couldn't pay my taxes, or I'd desperately plead with banks to release funds that hadn't cleared yet. When it came to money, I believed the IRS, banks and bill collectors were out to get me.

I played my role beautifully. Mainly because I didn't know this critical secret: Things improve dramatically when you give up the victimhood gig. Suddenly you wake up to a whole lot of bad choices you've made again and again. You can see them with your own eyes. And that's when everything shifts.

For me, I'd conveniently refused to look at the fact that I'd compulsively overspent, racking up credit card debts that lasted for decades. It got to the point that I was paying thousands of dollars in credit card interest every year.

It wasn't until I finally realized how out-of-control this was that I was able to get help. Finally, I could step up, take responsibility, and stop debting. I got rid of my credit cards altogether, and today my financial life is far more stable and under control. And I know when I need to ask for help.

When we start to look at our patterns, we realize much of our 'bad luck' is actually well under our control. This can be true about anything hard in our lives, from living with financial chaos to being in a toxic, bullying relationship.

The key is claiming that critical bit of responsibility for ourselves. And this means stepping into our power.

If we can allow ourselves to drop whatever story we're clinging to, and really, truly look at our situation, then we make discoveries. In the #metoo movement, women around the world have done this brilliantly, as they out the men who have sexually harassed and bullied them. They simply stopped buying into the silent social code that told them they had to put up with this treatment.

When we speak up and defend ourselves, we not only stop the abuse. We begin to forgive ourselves, as well. And that's when we develop some critical self-esteem.

Admitting my mistakes has been the hardest part for me. It was terribly embarrassing to own I had been a financial baby for much of my adult life. Which, of course, was the real reason I thought banks and the IRS were bullies.

Similarly, I had to let go of the story that my former partner was the real reason our great lesbian love affair didn't last. In my mind, she became the hella-tyrant, rife with psychoses, with whom I was trapped. It was all very dramatic and exciting—a non-stop whirlwind of adrenaline.

In reality, I was beyond checked out in the relationship. I ignored my impulses to leave again and again, pretending things were fine. Or worse, I would leave in a big showy swirl of dust. Then I'd come crawling back on my knees, begging to return. I kept making up excuses for my partner's erratic, controlling behavior, and for the pain I was in.

In reality, I couldn't stand the idea that I might actually be alone again. So I stayed. Again and again.

In Victimland, we either hang out in checked out numbness, insisting that everything is 'fine' as we come back for more. Or we are a teary mess a lot of the time, reinforcing our position that we are 'right' and that the other, our perpetrator, is wrong. Which they may be. Yet, chances are we have a role to play as well in the dysfunction.

The problem is that often we linger again and again, despite the abuse. Or we remain silent and put up with it, day after day. We tell ourselves we have no other choice, as we are bullied into silence or lose ourselves in our fears. Victims are trained to keep coming back for more, and so we play the part. At some level, we may even believe we either need or deserve that negative treatment, again and again.

If I could have told myself the truth in my relationship, I would have seen we simply weren't a good fit. And I would have left far earlier. Yet, I was wired to be a victim, and so I chose the much rougher, more damaging route for myself.

Teal was a recovering victim when she died. She became big on smashing the mindset wherever she spotted it. If I complained excessively about something on the phone to her, she'd chime right in with, "Yo! Mom! *Vic-tim…*"

Right, Teal. I hear you. These days I vote for reality and I take it as it comes.

No one has to be a victim in this sweet, short life we are given. Well, we can, of course, but why bother? Why not tell those bullies where to go? Why not stand up and refuse to be treated shabbily?

Or even better, why not just walk away when the situation merits it?

And while you're at it, why not choose joy instead?

Want to find out if you are a victim? Check out my 'Are You a Victim?' Questionnaire. (It just takes a minute!)
Go to: suzannefalter.com/victim

Getting Through the Pain of a Transition

Today I am in despair. There is no particular drama in my life—all my physical needs are well met. I feel loved by my friends and family. There is money in the bank. My health is fine, and I like where I live.

Instead…I am shedding. I am letting go of an old me that grew past her prime. My son has become an independent man who's thriving on the other side of the country. My daughter is a speck of dust in the Universe, a memory, a spirit who still drops in to dazzle me from time to time. My former husband of twenty-five years is living his own life, and I am living mine.

These people don't need me in the same way anymore. My days of being a van-driving, homework-helping, pie-making mom are over. As were the days of being a devoted, straight wife when I left my marriage to come out as a lesbian.

So…who am I then? This is the question all of us face when we are in the despair of transition.

A coach I know likens such change to a game of cards. She calls this phase the 'The Shuffle'—cards get dropped, passed back and forth, and generally mixed up by the hands of life. And that is just how it feels…turbulent at times, then strangely orderly.

I shed the small, masked self I was for most of my life—the daughter, wife and mother who defined herself through service, albeit with a career as well. In this way, I am learning to serve the least likely one of all…me.

My transition is a grand lesson in putting myself first. And honestly, I am just learning how to do this. If you grew up in a dysfunctional household with a needy mother like I did, your own needs were not well met. In fact, they just became dusty furniture in the house—always there and often ignored.

Then you grow up, emerge into adulthood, and a terrible realization hits you. You have no idea what your needs actually are. A much-desired pocket of time appears and you grab on to it hungrily… but then you can't decide how to fill it.

You feel half-sick and sad, so you climb into bed knowing there is something you need to do. But what? Journal? Cry? Eat chocolate? Call a friend? You know if you do nothing you will feel worse. Or perhaps you bury yourself in work, or shopping, or meds, or food so you don't have to notice those troublesome needs in the first place.

It's like your soul is buried under a thick sweater and perhaps a giant wool coat, too. It's back there somewhere, but you can't quite feel it.

Meeting your needs becomes a practice of continually scanning for clues…it's a practice that must be cultivated. So you begin by asking yourself questions. How do I feel today? What do I need right now? This practice requires becoming intentionally 'selfish'—that charged word from childhood. Then slowly, over time, answers present themselves as you learn to serve yourself, and the world, far more powerfully.

This is a process of becoming intimate with the Self, this unfolding into a new life. Acute attention is required. You must end the numbing, dulling behaviors that cloud your perception. Then you have to start trying on new systems of support and helpful resources, just like you would when you're shopping for clothes.

Bear in mind that all of this awkward discomfort and pain is necessary. The despair of shedding has to happen to make room for the new. There is a bigger plan, a brighter life, a stronger love, a more powerful calling just ahead. And to get there you must release the old patterns and the well-worn grooves that simply don't work any more.

Relax, trust, and feel your feelings, my friend…and then listen like you never have before.

Believe me when I tell you, everything is going to be okay… really.

What's Really Going on When Women Cry for 'No Reason'

I'm embarrassed to admit it, but going to church makes me cry. Like…every single time.

I stand there trying to sing a hymn, or I sit there listening to someone's poignant share about what their life is like.

And I weep. No matter how much I try to fight it, I cannot.

WTF, right?

Believe me, it's not that I'm suffering. I'm a perfectly happy person. These days there is nothing inherently 'wrong' in my life. It's just that I find myself crying at times. And damned if I know exactly why.

Is it my hormones? The phases of the moon? Or is it just one of those eternal mysteries, like the missing sock, that has no easy answer?

One minute I am fun, lively, capable and generally solving all sorts of problems. But the next thing I know I am sad and limp…a real wet dishrag…and for no apparent reason.

Speaking as a woman who finds her way to weepiness often, I believe I am not alone. I can still remember my mother crying into her perfectly prepared plate of dinner when I was a child. It was mystifying then, but now I understand.

It's not that there actually aren't enough hours in a day. There are and we know it.

It's that we can't live up to our own unreasonable expectations.

We can't always be that perfect mother, wife, sister, neighbor, community leader or career superstar we long to be. Nor can we fix this broken world by ourselves…and especially not all at once.

Teal used to call me up regularly so she could have a small meltdown. "Oh, Mom," she'd begin, her voice filling with tears. "I don't even know why I'm crying!"

In the last few years of her life, before her sudden death in 2012, we had an agreement in that she could call me up any time just to cry for no reason. We figured she was on schedule if she had a weepy meltdown about every two weeks.

Because sometimes, honestly, you just need to cry. But why? Here are a few ideas.

1. **We get tired of holding the world on our shoulders.** Yes, we do feel we must hoist it alone…even with a perfectly competent mate by our side.
2. **We care too much.** About our children, your children, our aging parents, plus our friends, colleagues, the homeless guy down the street and the neighbor's sister's cat. No one escapes our empathic radar. We just can't help it.
3. **We are all heart—and then some.** We tend to feel our way through life. So when we come a bit unraveled…well, we fall apart. It's that simple.
4. **There isn't enough time in life to get it all done.** So we slide into emotional overwhelm sometimes. That's when we long to be soothed with a pint of Ben & Jerry's served in a dark room.
5. **Someone still has to do the laundry.** Whether it is us, a helpful child, our spouse or the service we hired to do it, we still have to think about it. Along with several thousand other things, all of which are quietly nagging us…all the time…in the background.

This emotional landscape—just like our purses and backpacks—represents a crowded no-man's land packed with accumulated stuff.

There is just so much. How we long for someone (anyone!) to take it all away.

And that's about when we dissolve into tears.

The solution is to step away for a moment and fall apart, gently and willingly.

Simply allow all that emotion to come tumbling on through. Know that whatever the issue is, this, too, will pass. No matter how big or small, having a cry really will make it all better. For crying is actually the body's way of cleaning house.

I once met a photographer whose work was shooting tears microscopically. Happy tears looked completely different from the tears of grief or anxiety, she told me. In other words, your heart, your soul and your body know exactly what they are doing when you weep. And every last tear has been designed to give you what you need. So stop questioning and worrying.

Instead, start trusting your own beautiful process, and go ahead…sob if you want.

If anyone around you asks what is going on, just let them know what you need. Perhaps it's just a bit of warm appreciation, like a soft blanket of comfort. Perhaps an arm around the shoulders would do nicely, as well as a consoling word.

Sometimes all we need is someone to listen. Then, together, we can return to the heart of love, for isn't that what we are made of?

I invite you to think of your next weepy breakdown as a necessary pit stop for refueling.

No shame. No guilt. Just love.

Should You Quit Pursuing Your Dreams or Hang In There?

I've often written about how guided our dream pursuits can be, and how all you have to do is tune in to 'get the message' on what to do next. That said, what do you do when the Universe seems to be sending you mixed signals, i.e. You feel you're on the path. You're following all the signals, but somehow fiascoes happen. Things grind to a halt. Nothing moves ahead as planned.

Should you abandon your project or change it significantly?

While you're at it…just what *is* a signal from the Universe? And when are the thoughts in your head only your own resistance and fear? How do you know which is which?

I've given this matter a lot of thought, and put it through the filter of my own experience. There is indeed a light, grounded certainty to the messages from our inner guidance. They're quiet, confident and even a little surprising sometimes.

By contrast, when something pops up from our own striving consciousness, it often has a whiff of sweat to it. It requires I do a whole lot of activity with no clear path to results. It also has a ring of fear—as in, 'I'd better just do this to be on the safe side.'

Guided notions, especially those to abandon ship, have a different character altogether. Here's what I've determined are sure signs of a Universal signal telling you to change course:

1. **The signal is big and dramatic.** Back in my twenties, when

I was a freelance copywriter yearning to be a real writer, the Universe arranged for my copy portfolio to be stolen and my income stream to dry up overnight. Suddenly I was out of work and had plenty of time to finish my first novel. It got picked up by a major publisher within just a few months, and so I established myself as an author.

2. **Clues start piling up.** About ten years ago I put together a small cabaret trio to perform locally. I thought it would be a great way to keep my vocal chops up while developing a bigger, more long-term project for myself. Yet, within one twenty-four-hour span, one partner pulled out, the other decided she wasn't sure she wanted to stick with it, and the borrowed piano we'd been rehearsing with got loaned elsewhere. I got the message and let go.

3. **Your instinct confirms the signs around you.** As I was rehearsing with the ill-fated trio, collecting music, and lugging borrowed pianos around, I had this vague background sense that I should really put that energy into something I was writing. Still I chose to ignore it. Meanwhile, the Universe saw me busying myself with the wrong long-term project and let me know it.

4. **You get a great sense of relief when you follow the signs and let go.** I did, and so did my partners on that project. In no time, I was headed in the right direction, writing my first personal growth book.

5. **Sometimes, however, the obstacles you're running into are only your mind doing its Dance of Resistance.** This is particularly true when we are afraid—but we are drawn to a pursuit we know we simply must take on. If any of these ideas ring true, stay the course. Chances are there are lessons here.

6. **The problem is familiar.** It may be that you always seem to run out of money for your project, or you keep getting

sick. Somehow, trouble always happens when you aim for the exciting unknown. I used to get sore throats before I performed...mainly because I hadn't yet given myself permission to be a big, gutsy, great singer. A 'same-old-same-old' issue would NOT qualify as a sign from the Universe to change course. Instead, this is rich territory for lessons to emerge.

7. **There's a sense of straining or uncertainty to the signal.** You get a signal, but it's just not clear somehow. Instead, it's mushy and uncertain. It could be interpreted as a signal...but somehow, it's not. Notice that this 'signal' seems to mesh nicely with your rampant fear at moving forward, or your innate aversion to taking risks. Not a sign...just a wave of fear.

8. **You're missing key pieces of dream infrastructure.** You need the essentials first: support, organization tools, a balanced financial set up, and regular dream time in which to get things done. Remember that without these key pieces, no dream can move on as scheduled. First, put your house in order, then build the dream.

Hope this helps you discover the next right thing.

The Secret to Relaxing About Life

There is a strange paradox about life. Seldom is the one we are living the life we think we *should* be living.

Somehow we can never get quite enough money, or power or titles or sex or adventures or love or anything to truly feel we've got our share. Like hungry birds in their nests, our beaks are always open, demanding yet another worm. There is always some better position, some higher level of responsibility, some more exalted realm we think should be ours.

At least, this much has been true for me…until recently.

Not only did I consistently believe that I didn't have 'enough,' I believed that *I* wasn't enough either. I honestly thought that if I got that million-dollar book deal/perfect body/perfect…whatever… then I'd finally be whole and complete.

Then I could relax! Then I could be happy! I could stop pushing so hard and endlessly striving. Then, in the eyes of the Universe, Mom, and everyone else I would finally be enough. Or so I thought.

It was only as I approached the ripe old age of 60, that I finally decided to let go of this toxic illusion. This, right here and right now, is the life I've been given. And this, right here and right now, is as good as it gets.

What happened was that I was standing in our church singing in one of our annual concerts, singing my heart out with my fellow choir members. There was nothing slick or high visibility about the event. The audience was peppered with families and dotted with unruly kids and crying babies. We had a few microphones, and a very nice pianist, and that was about it.

There is also nothing slick about my life. My work continues along on a humble path. There is no massive book deal, no high visibility position, none of the things that I'd always imagined would make me happy.

But on that day, as I looked out over the crowd and sang, delivering my gift for that particular moment, I felt intensely bonded to each person sitting there. I could feel the love rising in the room, and the slightly sweaty, restless-child imperfection of all of it at the same time.

It was spectacularly beautiful.

These are my people, I thought to myself, *and I am in exactly the right place doing the right thing at the right time.* On the other side of the choir, my love was singing in the tenor section. We were experiencing the uplift of the music together, as our choir director beamed his approval.

Simply put, we were one with the audience, with each other and all the good and caring musicians gathered around us. That's when I understood, unequivocally, this is as good as it gets.

And that's when I saw the grand illusion that my long-held dream has been. As long as I quantify my life by many book deals, or income hikes, or vacations, or…whatever…I receive, there will probably never be 'enough,' not in this congested, tired little mind.

Furthermore, I will miss the deep and beautiful treasure of the life that's happening here and now.

I realize now that it's okay to have dreams and goals as long as they are accompanied by an intense sense of gratitude for what is present now—as long as I don't reject the reality of the present moment for some cherished illusion in my mind—because that illusion has no substance.

Down here, in the thick of life, only one thing counts and that is tapping into the love that is in this present moment. Whether you know it or not, that love does indeed surround you. By being grateful as we gaze ahead, we become hopeful again, and ready to be surprised by life.

Wherever you are, may you know that, today, right here and right now, you truly are enough.

In Praise of Reality and Why We Hide from It

I've been learning to stay awake. No, I'm not referring to getting past my need to be in bed by ten. I'm talking about the ability to stay conscious, present and tuned in to what is happening right here and right now. No matter what is going on.

I'm talking about not living in the suspended, sunlit world of fantasy when it comes to people, places and things. Instead, I'm learning to tell it like it is, mostly to myself.

Slowly and gently, I embrace reality.

Reality is not sexy and fun most of the time. It's gritty. It's disorganized, messy, and it often hurts. It also involves things like traffic, bad weather, disloyalty, unkindness, trauma and physical pain. Which is probably why people who have Near Death Experiences often want to stay on the other side.

And yeah, sometimes reality is euphoric, beautiful and sunlit, too.

The important thing is that reality is neither good nor bad, neither black nor white. Instead, it is a utopia of variety—an ever-changing kaleidoscope of sights, smells, and sounds all woven into the full range of emotional experiences from stinky to filled with Grace.

Which is gorgeous if you allow yourself to stay conscious.

Yet, if you took some physical or emotional hits as a child, you learned to ignore reality early on. Instead, you found yourself suspended in your own little hammock of make-believe. Your arguing, alcoholic parents were 'normal.' Your bullying siblings or classmates were 'just kids being kids.' You did your best to tune out the fights as well as those pesky feelings of yours.

And so you pushed on, determined to survive. Your own anguish and your inability to cope simply weren't allowed to exist—they couldn't. Because otherwise you figured you might die.

When you start to heal all these old wounds through therapy, support group work, spiritual work or Twelve-Step recovery programs, you notice an interesting thing.

You start to forgive yourself. And then…you start to forgive the players in your past. All of them. But you can't get there until you begin to disgorge the quantum pain that is lodged deep in your heart. And that happens by doing nothing more than feeling your feelings.

This is when embracing reality becomes not only possible…over time, it gets more comfortable. Then it becomes downright joyful.

The pain of recognizing discomfort and/or remembering past traumas can seem intolerable at first. Strange waves of grief come out of nowhere and deluge you. Sometimes you find yourself shedding rage, or the big one—fear.

If you can slow down and allow these ghost feelings to pour through you—for as long as it takes—they always, always clear. They must, for this is the law of all things. Sometimes they dissolve quickly and sometimes they take a while. But either way, they do eventually subside.

We only 'get stuck' when we lose faith, hold back in fear and refuse to allow nature to work its beautiful course.

We have hearts and souls that were designed to process pain efficiently, and so allow us to move in grace back to reality. So there is no need to hide in the thousand and one places the world provides—from Candy Crush and sexting to weed, jelly donuts, and Stoli martinis.

Instead, why not try becoming still and quiet just to see what is in there, asking for your attention? I promise that going through the pain of surrender is well worth the release that awaits on the other side.

Here is to your dose of courage, whatever it takes, to gently become present in the embrace of reality. May you, too, discover the magic that lives within your heart.

How to Stop Doing So Much and Start Receiving More

My beloved yoga teacher, Kashi, presented me with a challenge. At the time, I was trying to 'work' yoga in my life—pushing myself to the maximum all the time, sweating like a pig on my mat, heaving, grunting and striving to do more, more and even more. I mistakenly believed that the harder I pushed, the better my life would go. So it made sense to go for maximum form…right?

After all, I'd been making progress. Pretty soon I thought I might even be able to do a headstand—or even a handstand. I was getting pretty fired up thinking about myself as 'good' at yoga. Ah, but humility was at hand.

Kashi, in her wisdom, was having none of it. "Stop striving," she suggested. "Go for only seventy percent, instead of one hundred percent. It's part of letting go." To make her point, she also suggested I abandon my desire to be in her advanced class for the moment. "Really, you should go back to beginner," she said.

I was disappointed, but when I really thought about it, I could kind of see her point. Relaxing and going with the flow really *is* the easier, more cosmically in tune path. But the beginners class? That hurt!

Mercifully, my ego let me off the hook and I was able to take her advice. But it wasn't easy.

If you are like me, for most of your life you have had a relentless (and I do mean relentless) taskmaster in your head, commanding you ever forward. For many years, this quest for excellence was intrinsically linked to my survival. I had to be the uber-achieving child star, the great hope of the family.

Above all else, I was here to make my parents proud, so I had to get with the program. I believed that I must, at all times, deliver one hundred percent—ideally a little more, if possible. It appeared that undoing this thinking was Kashi's point.

Tentatively, day by day, I began to actually do a little less in my yoga practice. After all, I wasn't entirely sure I could trust this quest for non-perfection. Still I did it.

I did go back to the beginner class, and I relearned all the postures. I began to relax more about doing them as I went, and stopped trying to achieve. Repeatedly, I lay down and assumed the fetal rest position 'Child's Pose'—the universal symbol of 'I quit,' while everyone around me was going hard at it.

Still, thoughts swirled through my head.

What if I never get out of the beginner's class?

What if Kashi is right? What if I'm really powerless over making anything happen in life?

Who am I if I am not a 'human doing' as opposed to a human being?

So I began to undo the over striving that had marked so much of my life. Each day after yoga, I would go to my office and work only until I was mildly tired instead of dead exhausted, and permanently bent into 'chair shape.'

Then I began to just wander around with this new, unaccustomed time off. I felt aimless and slightly worried—I should be doing more! Right? And if I don't…will I *really* be provided for? Or has God gotten me confused with someone else?

The entire effort felt awkward in the beginning. Part of me simply didn't trust this seventy percent effort. A little voice in my head stamped her foot and said, "You can work all you want, honey, but you won't EVER be enough!"

Then I remembered that I actually did have enough in that exact moment—and the next, and the next. I kept being reminded as I went, day by day, that I actually was enough. I was becoming better than ever, in fact. How did I know this, you might ask?

When I really looked at it and told the truth, every last need of mine had been amply provided for since my life came crashing down around my ears in 2012. It was uncanny, actually. My business was over, and there was no income to speak of…yet strange things happened.

A relative died and a small inheritance appeared. An offer to write fiction for an investor came out of nowhere. People called me up asking me to speak about things that I never could have anticipated—for good money. It seemed the Universe really was nudging me back to my true work, writing and speaking, and so I followed.

Each day I just kept cultivating a practice of doing less, and going with the flow. I aimed for that precious 'just enough'—how I now began to consider Kashi's suggested seventy percent. And a remarkable thing happened in the process. I began to like myself a whole lot more.

For when we are constantly in overachieving and perfection mode, we can't ever give ourselves a break. And nothing really ever *is* good enough. But when we aim to do things more casually, we discover one of life's secrets…that by doing a little bit less you can fall in love with yourself again.

You begin to think of yourself with compassion, instead of rigidity and frustration. You love yourself more, and so you love the very process of living.

The Eight Secrets of Emotional Self-Care

As a thinking, feeling human, I've made a discovery. Yes, self-care is important. However, the self-care it seems we really need isn't just regular exercise, drinking smoothies, and getting massages.

What is truly critical to our well-being is emotional self-care. Because, basically, life is hard. That's why I've put together my own set of ground rules for better emotional self-care.

1. **Honor my feelings.** There's no getting around it. If I don't let my emotions cycle through me, I walk around feeling off. Then finally, I get to have that good cry and it's a relief. Turns out we are designed to constantly cleanse our psyches by allowing our emotions to move through us.

   Furthermore, when I delay, ignore or stuff my feeling, no one else gets to benefit either. Yet, this does not mean going off and dumping those emotions on someone else. (See # 2 below.)

   Our anger and our fear are here to protect us. So I'm learning to let them do their job.

2. **Remember it's all about mom.** We are always processing emotional sludge, most of which we think has nothing to do with us. But actually, all of it has to do with us—and the gigantic filters we have that constantly trigger memories from our past.

When something challenging or even joyful happens, old memories automatically pour through our subconscious. They can make us euphoric, just as they can render us mute with anger.

So the oversized, white-hot rage I feel when a car cuts me off is a flicker from my past. I can tell when I'm triggered because the event usually does not warrant the huge reaction I have.

Good self-care means gently reminding ourselves when we are triggered. Then allowing our feelings to flow when we're alone, until eventually they resolve.

3. **Become humble.** It's hard to be a humble human, and yet, when I am, I set myself free. Humility means I don't actually need to be perfect…nor do I need to be right.

In fact, I don't have to be anything other than just good old me, as I am right here and right now. Humility also means everyone else gets to be the equally flawed creatures they are, because basically we're all in this together.

4. **Know and express my boundaries.** Being clear on my boundaries and setting them is a lifelong learning for me. Sometimes I'm great at it. Other times, not so much. If we didn't get to have boundaries as kids, we have to learn to do this as adults.

The key is to honor our emotions and then find the courage to speak up kindly. Requests work well here.

If you feel shy about this, keep this in mind. I've discovered people appreciate when I am clear about my boundaries. Then they don't have to awkwardly wonder, guess or try to accommodate me somehow.

5. **Own my stuff…and nothing more.** Good emotional self-care includes only being responsible for 'my side of the street.' Those of us who come from abused backgrounds tend to say we're sorry a lot. And we take on everyone else's issues.

Yet, I don't have to apologize to someone who dumps on me for no good reason, and neither do you. That would be someone else's problem, not ours.

6. **Remember forgiveness sets me free.** That sticky pile of resentments I carried around most of my life? Turns out they're a massive energy suck, mainly because they contain a piece of me that's also waiting to be forgiven.

I've discovered that these conflicts are never one-sided. It takes two people to make a snit. But once I forgive myself *and* the other person, my heart can relax and my soul can breathe freely again.

7. **Stay out of harm's way.** Our emotions are always on, like finely tuned radar reading the people and places all around us, scanning for safety.

So it's worth noticing when I feel uncomfortable or even mildly frightened by someone else or the place I'm in. That's when I usually leave. Or, if I can't, I pull down my 'invisible shield.' That would be our inner protective armor, which is always at the ready, waiting to help.

And, yeah, I can still love someone, and even respect them, though I may not want to spend much time with them. (I'm thinking of difficult family members here.)

Our guidance system is always on for a reason.

8. **Be patient with myself.** Guess what? We are all works in progress until the day we die. But then, isn't the point of life to learn, evolve and grow?

That means I probably won't 'get it right' the first time, or maybe even the fiftieth, nor may you. But we may just nail it the fifty-first time.

In the end, it really all is about us and our tender hearts. If we really, truly show up and care for them, they will abundantly serve us in return.

Getting Out of the Cage of Self-Doubt

The image was frightening. Hannibal Lector's face, complete with face mask, peered out from inside a small cage. The metal bars covering his mouth glinted in the sun.

No, this wasn't *Silence of the Lambs 2*. It was my dream, and it annoyed the hell out of me.

Because for me, the message was clear: Stop locking yourself in a cage of your own making, refusing to be heard.

The previous day I'd been in a slump, damning myself for not being more productive, more inspired, more 'fire in the belly.'

Now in my seventh year of grief after the death of my daughter, now at the ripe old age of 60, I should be all better. Or so argues my mind.

I should be just like I was before her death—even though I am now a significantly different, older person, and even though my life has been profoundly changed.

Somehow it feels like my current level of productivity is not enough. Enter Hannibal Lector.

When you suffer a shocking loss, you grow and evolve differently as a result. You can't help but be changed by it, and perhaps that is the point. For what is life but a non-stop series of tumbles, splats, triumphs and recoveries?

This is how we learn.

Furthermore, we are designed to take big hits, so if we choose we can rise up again. Still we won't ever be the way we once were. Nor should we be. We will be altered forever by our misfortune, and hopefully become wiser as a result.

For me, I am definitely humbler. I don't need to wave flags and get all eyes in the room on me anymore. And my spirituality has grown deeper and far more connected. Part of me no longer cares about my prospects for success, either.

Yet at the same time I often feel like I just don't quite measure up.

My mind wonders…*is this softer, gentler me who lacks ambition really okay?*

Is it alright, after years of grief, to not need to burn up the world anymore? My needs are met. I have everything I could possibly ask for.

So is this life I'm living actually enough, right here and right now? Even in this driven world of striving and ambition?

At such times I always come back to an important set point. There are only two things that matter to me now. Self care, which includes the deep love I share with my wife, and my call to become a better person and share that path, step by step, with my readers.

But when I'm locked in my cage of self-doubt, I forget all of that. Then nothing I've done seems significant at all. The Buddhists say I'm at choice here. I can give in to the voice of *dukkha*, or 'unsatisfactoriness,' in my head and really milk it for all it's worth. Or I can just observe it, acknowledge it and let it go.

It's sort of like turning off the current state of politics, and deciding I don't need all that negativity in my head.

So I am cultivating a practice of letting my feelings of weakness simply be. Because that's all they are—just feelings and nothing more.

They are not a pronouncement about my worth in the world. They aren't predictors of my future. And they certainly aren't reliable signposts.

For this, too, will change. Today I might feel weak and indecisive. But tomorrow, I could get a whole new outlook on life. We are always in flux and that is an exciting thing. We never really know what could happen next.

What's important today is to forgive myself for not being as 'on' as I once was. I need to give myself a compassionate pat on the back, and allow myself to do what I can comfortably do…expecting nothing more.

Then, magically, I *am* enough and the cage door swings slowly open. So I emerge once again, ready, willing and able to help.

Ironic, isn't it?

But then isn't this the sweet process of life as it unfolds, one day at a time, ever pushing us forth to become better, humbler, kinder… the embodiment of love.

The Five-Minute Antidote to Your Fear

There came a time not long ago, when I felt like I was on top of the world. My work was going well, my relationship even better—I had a spring in my step as I climbed out of bed each morning. I simply couldn't wait to unwrap another excellent day.

But now it's another story.

Today I am fresh out of minor surgery, which means I'm limping around with a black plastic 'boot' on my foot. I feel immensely sorry for myself. I'm also battling some age-old demons in my head as I launch my first novel in twenty-five years.

I feel vulnerable, weak and afraid.

So when am I going to get this right, this slippery, disorganized thing called life? When am I going to finally dissolve into that place on the horizon where money and health are abundant, the weather is always excellent, and me and my pals are relaxed *and* have plenty of time to chat?

Oh yeah…that would be never. Sometimes I just forget.

The Buddhists say this is one of the Four Noble Truths—the notion that *there will be suffering*. They even have a name for it: *Dukkha*.

Dukkha is all about craving and clinging, and wishing that things were any other way than how they are at exactly this moment. And if I think long and hard enough, and listen to the sweet consolation of my love as she encourages me, I finally get the point.

Dukkha is actually a critical part of life. And why, you ask? So you and I can get over it, basically, and thus move forward. Which is another one of the Four Noble Truths; *there is an end to suffering*. We simply must do the work necessary to get there.

I'm not a practicing Buddhist, and I doubt I have the subtleties right here. But I do know when Life presents me with one of her lessons, and that would be now.

The mad, deep fear I keep feeling in my gut comes from long ago. I had an ambitious father who wanted me to be a star, and a mother who was competitive, jealous and wanted me to stay in the background. Though they are both dead, they have been duking it out in my head for decades now.

The beautiful thing is that now I know when they're at it again.

So…*yes*…I *am* going to feel afraid when I launch books and emerge into the spotlight. Yet, at the same time, here I am laid up and unable to move around much at all. So I have plenty of time to contemplate the blank screen, and chip away at my endless list of book promotion tasks.

They go together rather neatly, don't you think?

It's as if Spirit just couldn't resist the chance to help me really live into that old fear of mine—and do something about it. Which is exactly the way I resolve such conflicts.

Where I'm heading, ideally, is detachment; that divine state of nothingness in which I crave nothing more than doing the next right thing.

In such a simple, joyous place, I imagine I won't feel beholden to any agenda at all. I'll be in happy free-flow all day long, taking the path one step at a time. Do you know that essential place of bliss I'm talking about?

There is no second-guessing, no doubting and shame. There is no wallowing in stories, or peeved fist-shaking at the past. Instead, there is a simple, gracious focus on what is, right here and right now.

I can do this in this moment. And actually, so can you. All we have to do is look at our fear and get clear on what it is—a ghost from the past, here to taunt us, and even remind us to get to work. And then we have to surrender to it.

It's a fact; there will be suffering. So why resist?

When I remember this, I can forget about the saga of my Achilles tendon and get busy creating the next right thing. I can take three deep breaths and refocus my attention as I choose, very intentionally, on what to do next.

I can forget all about my little dramas and let the next moment unfold, held once more in the lovely grace of divine flow.

What can you do right now to dissolve your own web of tension? Consider this: What next right thing can you relax into?

This moment—right here and right now—is yours for the taking. So may this be your invitation to take it.

Why not seize it…here and now?

How to Move on When the Time is Right

Have you ever had the feeling that there is a next step for you to take, perhaps even a big one, but you have no idea how and when to do it?

That's been my experience lately. It's been more than some years since the death of my daughter, and I have slowly and powerfully moved through my grief…or at least most of it.

I no longer fall apart at the mention of her name. I have energy again, and have stopped feeling like I live in a heavy cloud of uncertainty all the time.

I keep thinking it is time for me to work longer and harder, and produce more to be of real service in the world. There are things to do, my busy mind tells me. A podcast and a memoir need to be finished. A course needs to be set up. And another novel needs writing. And yet…

I hang back.

At such times, I still cling to the sweet, warm sanctuary of my grief.

How can I step out into the world again as I once did, now that I am truly vulnerable? My turtle shell of defensiveness and ambition are simply gone. I am raw, exposed, and as I get older, so much less driven.

My only ambition now is to serve God's will…yet that will does seem to be nudging me right back to where I came from. So how do I proceed?

With caution, by taking my time? Or with abandon, throwing myself into my work once again? Perhaps this is just an uncomfortable 'hump' I have to force myself over.

This is where Teal's Goddess Cards come in. At the end of her life, she relied heavily on Doreen Virtue's *Goddess Guidance Oracle Cards* to help her navigate times like this. So recently, I pulled out her beautiful, worn box of cards.

Shuffling the deck, I focused on my question: 'Should I push myself to be more productive again?'

I pulled three cards and lay them on my desk. The card on the left was all about my immediate past.

Not surprisingly, the goddess pictured here was Ishtar. "Boundaries," read the card. It advised me to respect my own time and energy enough to know when to say 'no' to others. A note also cautioned against doing things out of guilt or obligation.

It was an apt description of where I had been with my grief for several years.

The middle card, which showed my current situation, pictured the goddess Ostara, for 'Fertility.' This one was all about diving into new projects, and exploring new possibilities. Notably, the card was upside down, meaning I had work to do here.

Okay, so I was meant to proceed with the projects that had been on my mind. But…how?

The card I'd just looked at noted that in that process I'd create some new infrastructure—or ways to be supported.

Perhaps that meant I needed to create better working conditions for myself. Like not doing things simply to make income, but doing them instead through divine flow. That seemed right. This could be work marked by a happy sense of 'rightness,' ease and inspiration, instead of guilt and obligation.

This would be work done because inherently it feels good.

And that would mean trusting my process, and knowing all is moving ahead just as it is meant to. After all, my needs were well taken care of every minute since Teal's death. Again and again, I found myself with abundant time, money, health, friends…even overflowing love. I have truly wanted for nothing.

The only time that has not been the case was when I ignored my own guidance, and attempted to push myself to work.

So why on earth am I pushing myself so hard now?

The third card I pulled, indicating what lies ahead, said it all. The goddess pictured here was Maeve, who represents "Cycles and Rhythms." She advised me to listen to my body—which has always been Teal's message in spades.

Wow. The light now dawned brightly, with celestial choirs chiming in from above.

There *is* a right time to everything, and the natural cycles of my energy and emotions will deliver me to the perfect moment for creating the podcast, the memoir, the novel, and the courses. I really got this now.

I don't have to forge ahead just for the sake of forging ahead. That will help no one, least of all me.

Furthermore, I must not rush the flow of the Universe. Instead, I can join with it in an easy dance informed by love for myself and the world, and honor the notion of right timing.

This is how we create in gentle wholeness, consciousness and well-being. For there is no 'there' to get to, my friend. There is only the whole and healthy living of each day, each minute, to the best of our abilities. Turns out it's all pretty simple, huh?

May you and I both move through our lives in ease today…and every day.

How to Walk Away from 'Should'

Lately I've been pondering how important our thinking process is to our mental and physical wellbeing. I'll share a personal example to show you what I mean.

This afternoon, I have a choice. I can sit dutifully at my desk until 5 PM, and work on learning how to use my new screenflow software. Or…I can finish a blog up, ditch that project, and head off into nature.

Neuroscientists say that when I get up to Redwood Park for a walk with my wife and our dog, my tendency to ruminate (i.e. think negatively or fret about my past, or my life, or my business… or whatever) will decrease significantly.

The activity in the part of my brain associated with anxiety and depression will stop. All just because I'm taking a stroll in the park. Researchers have found that walking in nature, versus in a city, dramatically decreases this kind of negative thinking, while it increases creativity.

On the other hand, if I stay at my desk, and crank along on the screenflow training, one more item gets ticked off the list. At the end of which I'll be REALLY ready for that nice cold Friday night glass of Sauvignon Blanc. Because by then I'll be tired.

Too tired.

I'll be looking for ways to relieve the now present stress and pain of overwork, instead of feeling fresh and revived by a wonderful afternoon among the redwoods. In other words, I either choose a remedy…or I choose a preventative move towards wellbeing.

In the end, I choose wellbeing, because here's the thing. After a bunch of good, healing weekend R&R, I'm probably going to be totally into learning the rest of that training.

Which I'll do more efficiently and more happily with fresher, livelier brains. The only thing stopping me is my ability to step away from the 'shoulding' and the shame, and give myself what I need in the moment.

For me, right now, that means getting over my habitual tendency to overwork, and taking a walk.

In the past, that behavior was rooted in a need to prove myself—to be everything to everyone by accomplishing things. And yet, it turns out I'm only one person, and imperfect at that.

When my daughter died, all that unnecessary ambition and striving died right along with her. Suddenly I landed soundly on my ass in the land of crisis. I had to spend a lot of time slowly calming down, and then grieving, and then *very* slowly—over the course of four years—reinventing my life.

As a result, things are in balance now. And it is much, much easier to walk away from, say, screenflow training.

When you finally are at a place where you can listen to yourself, hear your needs and respond to them, you can begin to cycle back to a place of balance. Of alignment. This is really the crux of good self-care.

But all too often we lose ourselves in our shame, or perhaps the distraction of perpetual stimulation, from our work to the ever present phones in our hands. Why not take a look and see if there's something you'd rather let go of, instead of pushing yourself to do against all odds?

Are you listening to the phantom voices of past experience, or the wise voice of Now, Present and You? Believe me, she's always there and she always has something to say. You just need to tune in and listen.

May you walk away from work at just the right time, or whatever has used enough of your energy.

Then…why not? Go enjoy yourself!

Discovering That I Am Worth It

Perhaps the reason for all of this—the trauma suffered, the shock recovered, the falling apart and the knitting back together again—was simply so we can learn this truth: That we really are worth far more than we realized.

I am just starting to grasp this. And this beautiful self-awareness lives in the small minutes of the day—like surrendering to an excellent piece of music, or deciding to wear pink and a lot of lace just because I want to.

At the end of the day, these are the moments that define us.

I am worthy. I get it now. That awareness is like a gentle blooming in my soul—a waking up. It is a coming to terms with the extraordinary abundance in life.

You wouldn't expect such an outcome from a death as senseless as Teal's. But then, why wouldn't you? Because when God strikes in such untoward ways, life gets turned on its ear. And so we get to look at its underbelly, right there, undeniably exposed in front of us.

Which makes things like Teal's death far from senseless.

I know that underbelly intimately now. I've been lying right next to it, cheek pressed tight, smelling its earthy funk and realizing moment by moment that I am no longer afraid of it. In fact, there is something important and real about this underbelly. It seems to hold answers.

And so I have spent the better part of the last year working my way through all of these questions—the questions of an entire lifetime. As if the rest of my life will be a beautiful work of art, dedicated to her memory. So I figure I'd better make it the very best it can possibly be. This includes surrendering completely to joy.

I have no choice. God is looking me square in the face, and so I must comply. And I have succeeded in getting back to this place of recognition, this understanding of my own worthiness.

I know this is so because of something that just happened. When a bat woke me from my sleep recently I found myself in a medical dilemma. The Public Health protocol is to administer the rabies vaccine, in the event that (a) the bat bit you and (b) you didn't know it because you were asleep. And oh, yes, (c) chances are the bat might be rabid.

The rabies vaccine, a once draconian measure that included 16 excruciating shots into the abdomen, has improved. But like all things medical in America the price is exorbitant. I found it would cost more than my entire insurance deductible for the year, and mostly due to a single five-thousand-dollar shot into the site of the bite upon arrival at the Emergency Room.

Mind you, the bat may not have bitten me at all. But if it did, (leaving its tiny, barely detectable, mosquito-like bite)…and it was rabid…well, I'm dead. After a whole lot of frothing at the mouth. And that's just for starters.

P.S. According to *The Washington Post* the shots make you feel like lying on the couch for three weeks in a fluish stupor.

So I prayed about this. Was I 'worth' five thousand dollars, plus a whole lot of pain and suffering?

It was as if Spirit was testing me. Was I ready to declare my worth in monetary measure? And was I worth the piece of mind the vaccines would bring?

At first, I went with my old instincts; I ignored the whole thing. Because my default setting was historically one of lack, deprivation, and not getting my needs met. Then a friend who worked for Public

Health brought up the protocol. "You might want to get them," she advised.

I hemmed and hawed for two days, going back and forth over the pros and cons. Finally I started making calls to the Public Health department. And once again, God guided me.

I found a physician's assistant in the local hospital who was a knowledgeable expert on rabies. As I collected more and more facts, I felt like a parched traveler in the desert, heading straight for the oasis.

Yet in the end, I was still confused. Part of me wanted to stay stuck in the old paradigm, toughing it out, refusing help. Blowing off the whole thing. Then I started calling friends for advice, and that's when everything came apart. My friend Maureen put it simply, "If you go to the hospital, don't go alone."

Oh for God's sake! I thought…*Okay! Fine! I'll surrender! I'll just do the damn thing. But I'll be damned if I take anyone with me, because I'm a tough guy.*

Or so I thought.

Maureen's words rung through my head after I hung up. 'Don't go alone.' The thought flustered me. I couldn't possibly ask someone to go with me…could I? What would be in it for them? How could I presume that someone would do this just for me?

Wasn't I capable of doing this alone?

Well, of course I was. But having someone there was the sort of support I would never have asked for in the past. I set off for the hospital willfully alone. But then halfway there, I turned around and went home.

I pulled into my driveway and started calling people. Two were not home. Good.

I could do this alone. I'd always done these things alone.

I flipped back to a text I'd gotten earlier from my housemate, Yang Ming, asking me what I was doing that afternoon. Yang Ming is a twenty-seven-year-old Chinese-American, a dear soul with a young heart. She had a day off from her job.

Yang Ming offered to go with me. Yet, I hesitated. I couldn't ask her…could I?

And that's when my fears began to flood me, and so I dissolved into tears. I was scared. I did need help, and it was indeed safe to ask a good friend. And she agreed, God bless her.

By 4:30 Yang Ming and I were navigating the corridors of the hospital. By 5:00 an ER doctor determined I did not need the five-thousand-dollar shot but only the far less expensive vaccine. By 5:45 we were on our way to have Pho, my arm only slightly sore and the shot nothing more than a pin prick.

Just having Yang Ming's reassuring presence there beside me was comfort enough. And so the greatest lesson was learned—that I am worth caring for intimately. And that there are others in my world who would like nothing more than to offer support.

"I mean, you'd do this for me, right?" asked Yang Ming as we made our way back out through the hospital labyrinth.

Yes, my dear, yes. With all my heart.

How a Career Full of Failures Taught Me About Real Success

Have you ever noticed that our path in life is often to go through pain and suffering, connect the dots, and emerge a better person?

At least, that's how it seems to me. What I notice is that now, into my sixties, I am no longer struggling to 'make something BIG happen.' I already did that, albeit in my own small way.

It's official. I can relax now.

From as early as I can remember, I often had the thought that I must become a star—that my life depended upon it. So I went to the best college I could, worked my ass off in job after job, and married a man who I knew would boost me along. I also avoided my lesbianism like the plague, convinced it wouldn't help me.

Instead, I strived, pushed, and cajoled the Universe. And I had some small success. As I turned thirty, I published a first novel with a major publisher, which at the time felt like a crowning achievement. "This is it!" I thought with glee. "I'm gonna be famous for sure!"

I wasn't. My mother and fifteen of her friends bought my book. Despite my best efforts, my writing career didn't take off. So I tried again, this time with non-fiction.

I felt spiritually swept along as I followed the up-up-up trajectory of my first self-help book, *How Much Joy Can You Stand?*

This time is REALLY it, I told myself.

Again, I was wrong. Or perhaps…I was right. The book found

its path, I got a nice advance, and it sold tens of thousands of copies overall. Not stellar, but not bad.

Stardom, however, still had not arrived.

Life pushed me along to other arenas where I might 'be a star.' In my late forties, I went out on the road with a one-woman show. I simply had to use my other talents, I thought. And after all, I was a trained singer and actor. *That ought to do the trick*, I thought, figuring I'd simply been barking up the wrong creative tree. But it didn't.

While they loved me in Orlando, the rest of the tour was not a success. Houses were sparse; reviews were non-committal. I even tried to force the joy at one festival by getting friends to vote my show in as 'Best Comedy.' The win felt so empty and meaningless that I never even picked up my trophy.

The final straw came in Vancouver when a reviewer wrote that my show was the worst she'd ever seen, likening me to William Hung from American Idol. An audience member even walked into the middle of the stage during one of my monologues and triumphantly cried, "I am going to bring this show *down!*"

It turned out folks in Vancouver didn't get my sense of humor. So I hung up my wig and pushed on bravely, this time to Internet marketing. Here would-be stardom wasn't hard to create. I was an old marketing hack from days gone by, having served in ad agencies in my twenties. I just had to throw myself into it, work my ass off, and believe in the mission with all my heart.

Again, good things happened. I earned surprising amounts of money in a relatively short time, and suddenly people seemed to know me on the Internet. But when I poked my head up from time to time and looked around, it all felt empty and meaningless. Even this, with its abundant financial windfall, wasn't enough.

After nine years I let go of my marketing career and walked away, exhausted and entirely burned out. This was only a month before my daughter died. The day after her death, I found myself writing, simply because I had to. This, I knew, was a place where I could tread water safely until the 'next big thing' came along.

But in fact, I was giving my heart and soul exactly what I needed as I navigated this huge hole that had just been torn in my life. I didn't ask why I should write, nor what it would get for me. Nor did I worry about results. Instead, I simply felt my way along, writing my life, one essay at a time.

Since then things have slowly progressed. Two years after Teal's death, an investor approached me to write fiction, which then produced several series of independently published novels. Slowly, I also reclaimed the copyright on my self-help titles formerly published with major publishers, and I republished them as well.

Along the way, I've also written hundreds of essays simply because this is how I make sense of life now. I blog and I podcast, and so I understand. It's a simple equation, and the world seems to be in sync with this new, simple trajectory. Those essays on my blog attracted the interest of an agent, who encouraged me to write a memoir about my experiences since Teal died, particularly a book about how I learned self-care.

A major publisher then offered me my first book deal in fifteen years. It's a modest deal that I couldn't make a living from, and yet… audiobook rights and translation rights began to sell. And I began to understand there is a vision behind this work.

It's no longer driven by artificial dreams of being known by people—but instead, it's fueled by a sincere desire to connect with the world, share my ideas, and also Teal's legacy of healing. For in each of these books, and in many of these podcasts and essays, I share some of the hundreds of channeled bits of wisdom Teal received in her meditations.

They are insights that have helped put me right. And so, truly in flow, I have emerged to share them. At the same time, I have let go of the need to succeed. I suspect if I sent this organic, simple trajectory in to my college alumni magazine, I wouldn't dazzle the crowd. I'd be way back there behind the presidents of banks, the global politicos, and the doctors and lawyers.

Yet, perhaps this is the point…

What I know now is that I no longer have to be a star. I no longer have to have all the answers or do things perfectly. I don't even have to make a lot of money to feel satisfied. This simple, beautiful life—in which I am truly mistress of my own domain, living happily and doing what I love—is certainly enough.

Honestly, what more could any of us ask for beyond self-acceptance? So I have come to realize I actually am enough. It's kind of crazy, but it's true.

What matters now are the intangibles like the beautiful curve of my wife's hand as it lies on the bed sheet in the morning. Or the lovely glow of the winter sky at dawn outside our window. What matters is how happily the dog moves down the street on her walk, and what I will say next as I approach another blank page.

In the end, we simply have to show up, do the job God has given us to do, and love our fellow humans. That's enough. We don't have to push and strive endlessly, and make ourselves crazy in the process.

It is not our job to save the world or be a highly lauded hero. It's just to move through our days with love and grace, taking care of ourselves along the way.

We can only do what we can do, and nothing more. The old parable is true. The journey really isn't about the results. So life becomes simple again and the heavy cloak of brilliance gets lifted.

You and I are enough, right here and now, with not a thing added.

You can hear Suzanne's podcast, Self-Care for Extremely Busy Women, *on all popular podcast platforms including iTunes and Stitcher. You can read her blog at suzannefalter.com*

How I Learned to Stop Fighting and Heal My Anger

I'm a very nice person…perhaps too nice sometimes. And truthfully? Underneath that well-groomed, well-behaved exterior, a tiger lies in wait.

The fact is I can get angry. Very angry. So I've had to learn how to work with the behemoth that is my anger.

Here's how it goes.

Someone around me is having a bad day, or maybe a particularly harried moment. They snap. My hackles go up, and I snarl back. But then—instead of storming out, or allowing the moment to escalate into a back and forth that becomes an invective-hurling tirade—I retreat.

Or at least I try to.

I take myself off to another room, I close the door, and I do something I've found to be immensely helpful. I ask myself what's going on.

In those tense moments, it's so very easy to imagine the issue rests entirely with the other one. My mind can so easily spin and snap. *How could she say that? What exactly did he mean?*

I understand that I am the one who's having the big reaction. Psychotherapists would say I am triggered.

Rather than being able to calmly let the other person just have his moment, and give him a compassionate reply or a sympathetic pat on the shoulder, I have to run down memory lane. In a nanosecond, my psyche replays all the times I felt shamed, or afraid, or bullied, or abused.

So instead of being present in the moment with that slightly grumpy person, I'm back in sixth grade, being humiliated in the girl's locker room. Or my long-dead mother is standing in front of me shaking her finger, telling me how selfish and impossible I am.

The path back to shame and anger is so well-worn, I just have to go there.

And yet, there *can* be course correction.

What I've come to realize is that when I'm triggered, the other guy seems patently wrong. Just wrong…no matter what. My oversized upset is usually far bigger than the situation merits. Which is why holding my tongue and retreating is such a good idea.

Once I'm alone, the first thing I do is allow myself to feel as upset, outraged, fearful and bewildered as I want. I give myself a break—knowing that this psyche has some dings, and that I will eventually work my way back to a calm frame of mind.

I also remind myself that moments like these are inevitable… and that I can learn from them every time.

Instead of spinning endlessly through the story of what just occurred, I take a tender look back into my past. Sometimes I can even remember a similar time from childhood when I felt so powerless, or vulnerable, or afraid.

If I need to have a cry, I do. Or perhaps I do a little journaling in the moment. Either way, I sit with my feelings until I feel myself calm down.

Then, most importantly, I remind myself not to take the other person's upset personally. Sometimes, this is the hardest thing to do—because like I said, that path of shame and rage is well-worn. And somehow, part of me is always itching to travel it.

The truth is that the other person's upset probably has nothing to do with me. Chances are that she also feels horrible in that moment.

And, of course, I need to clean up where necessary. Did I cause some harm here? I open my eyes and take a good hard look, because I also know this: I am imperfect—and I'm going to make a lot more mistakes in my lifetime.

If there is some personal responsibility I need to take or an apology I need to make, I do it immediately. A clean slate also helps my psyche stay calm and relaxed.

The bottom line is this: When we own our anger—really own it, by sitting with it and even exploring it—we can heal it. These days I'm not as angry as I used to be. Instead, I find myself getting humbler and humbler.

Each time I sit with my triggers, I understand just a wee bit more about this complex, crazy creation that is me.

So my tiger is learning how to lie down and relax.

And that makes life all the sweeter.

The Thirty-Minute Exercise That Helped Me Forgive and Forget

There are people in this life who make me weary.

You know who I mean—the lover who discarded me, the boss who denigrated me, even the kids who relentlessly bullied me in grade school. For many years, there was an entire cast of characters in my psyche I thought I was done with.

Except that I wasn't. They still chimed in from time to time, simply as disembodied voices in my head. And why? Because again and again, I invited them in.

The truth is I longed to let them go. Fie on those bully kids and that impossible-to-please boss. And what about the toxic lover? I longed to get rid of her, too!

How I craved some much-needed space in my head. Once I had it, then I knew that all kinds of kind, lovely, nourishing things could grow in my mind instead.

So I decided to set these angry rants free.

A book I was reading at the time suggested it would be as simple as writing a letter to each person I was still resentful with. I would never send the letter, of course, but instead simply write it. And that alone would free up space in my heart.

Okay. Fair enough. At this point, it was three years after the toxic relationship, thirty-one years after the obnoxious boss, and forty-six years after the bully kids…so why not let it all go? Hadn't those negative voices occupied my head for long enough?

I sat down to write each person a letter and a very surprising thing happened. I began with my former lover, a person I felt had done me wrong in many, many ways. I felt damaged, injured, furious really. I really let it all hang out as I wrote.

Spiritual bypass was not allowed—I scrawled every last one of my petty, crude, pissy thoughts down on paper. I gnashed my teeth. I told her exactly what I thought of her…and then half way down the page, the tone suddenly shifted.

All of the sudden a small awareness of my role in the relationship crept in, and slowly it became clearer. I found myself writing, "Of course, I invited you into this dynamic by being a vacant, pliable victim…so we acted out our little drama just like actors in a play."

Whoa. *Really?*

Yes, really. The fact that I was being so nakedly honest gave me no recourse but to be honest about my own responsibility, as well. Did she mistreat me? Did she use me? Did she manipulate and control me?

Absolutely! And did I manipulate her right back?

I certainly did.

Every time I was silent and let my former lover abuse or control me, I fed our off-kilter dynamic. Every choice I made that didn't serve me merely cemented the unhappy lockstep we both found ourselves stuck in.

As I continued to write my letter to her, I discovered what a great thing our break-up was. It was actually a huge relief when she dumped me. And now, in writing this letter, I could see how critical this relationship was to my personal growth.

As a direct result of that break-up, I found my way into recovery work that helped me become humble again. I learned to live in a far healthier way and found a new, far deeper connection to God.

Out of the wreckage of this relationship, I also found the truly happy, deeply loving marriage I am now in. Mainly because I saw clearly where my defects of character were, and I set about owning them…and correcting them.

Our greatest teachers often show up as irritants in the path—the rock around which we must flow. The bully kids taught me to protect myself in situations that were unsafe. Not long after I left that school, I learned to run toward the people I resonated with, and to leave the rest to their own devices.

The obnoxious boss taught me how low my standards were, and how to aim higher with the next job I got—and then the next, and the next one after that.

Again and again, life conspires to bring the very best teachers our way, whether we like them or not. I say our souls demand it—for how else can we really grow?

By finally telling the truth, I owned the entire picture of what had happened. Here was my safe forum to truly express myself, and so discover the lessons buried behind the grief. Now I found I truly was ready to let go of the hurt, the pain and the anger.

At the end of the letter to my ex, I was filled with compassion, empathy and even gratitude for this remarkable woman I had once loved. I knew that part of me would even love her for years to come, whether or not we ever spoke again.

I had been reborn—because of one small, thirty-minute exercise.

If you are carrying resentment toward anyone in your life or your past, why not lay your burden down? You don't need to get them involved—you can truly do this all by yourself. All that you will lose is the artificial crutch of your resentment.

There is an innate joy that awaits all of us. It lives on the other side of humility, honesty and willingness.

I invite you to write a letter of your own—a letter you never send. For, if nothing else, it will be an act of total self-care.

How to Give Yourself the Pep Talk You Deserve

Okay, everyone, repeat after me:
We are good and wonderful people—even when we feel like hell.

I woke up with the blues the other day, and had a profound experience of finding my way back to some good and loving self-kindness. What it took, first of all, was letting go of the need to be blue. Putting aside that automatic desire to curl up and lick my wounds. Because let's face it, sometimes we actually want to play the victim—even when we know it's a pretty lame place.

Here are the steps I took to get a grip once more. May they serve you well the next time you've hit a wall.

1. **Call a friend.** Really, we were never meant to slog through this life alone—whether we are with a soul mate or not. Furthermore, those who care about you do want to help. So resist the urge to go off and lick your wounds alone. Generally that just makes things worse, right?
2. **Remember you have no perspective.** It's your life, so generally you can't see the forest for the trees. Just like Mark Twain thought *Huckleberry Finn* was a piece of trash, and Michelangelo remarked, after finishing the Sistine Chapel, "I am no painter." If you doubt your self-worth, keep in mind your perspective is not reliable. (Then see #1 above.)
3. **Expect the occasional s**tstorm.** Because that's how life is.

You will know suffering just as you know joy—even sometimes at the same time. Not only is suffering a reliable life experience, but it will ultimately become your most powerful teacher. Because that's how it is in this mortal coil.

4. **Know you will be fine.** Think about it. Even when times were bleak, you came out of it okay, if a bit dinged up. You always have been fine, and you always will be. And then one day you'll die. Job completed. Mission accomplished. Discomfort inevitably leads to something better.

5. **Expect a miracle (or ask for one.)** Even if you don't believe in a great spiritual organizing principle in this life, why not give it a whirl? No matter what, your mind will be soothed, your body will relax, and you will feel protected. Which ultimately leads to…yes…miracles.

6. **Ask for guidance to 'Bless it or Block it.'** This is a little trick a friend showed me who has a profound faith in a higher power that guides us all. When you are really feeling uncertain about which course to take—or so scared you literally can't take the next step—ask Spirit to bless or block your endeavor. The answer usually follows.

7. **Remember the stuff that is working in your life.** Somewhere in your dark stew of an existence, there are soft, clear, sweet places. Perhaps that's a beloved friend, or a special place that makes you feel wonderful. Maybe even a treasured letter or photograph, or possibly your work, or your health, or your kids. Whatever's working, name it now. Thank it profusely for being in your life. Then see if that doesn't give you a bit of a shift.

8. **Know that this, too, will pass.** Tomorrow you will wake up with two-hundred-thirty-two billion new cells in your body. That, alone, is reason for hope. Your life is constantly changing and evolving toward what is just ahead. So this place you're in right now? By tomorrow, it'll probably be gone.

9. **Above all, believe in your own perfection.** Yes, you are already perfect, just as you are, and this experience or uncertainty or doubt or dilemma is perfect, too. Easy for me to say, right? Yes! And…it's all happening for a reason.

The key is to trust that you have everything you need, here and now, to resolve anything you must resolve.

Not only do you have everything, you *are* everything. You were born whole and complete, and you will die whole and complete. We really were designed to be enough, and have enough, every minute of every day. *Even when it doesn't feel like it.*

Once you even begin to wrap your head around this truth, the next one falls neatly into place.

10. **Give back and know peace.** The ultimate game changer is service, given from the heart. What is your special gift you could give someone today? This essay is mine.

What's yours?

Go and give it. You will be so glad you did.

How to Find the Lessons Hidden in Everyday Dilemmas

By now, we're catching on: A life in crisis can be a fantastic teacher. There's nothing like a complete reset to wipe you clean, right? As you are dumped on your butt, you have no choice but to look around and reach for solutions. Which is how a lot of lessons get learned.

Yet…at the same time…what if a gentler sort of lesson-learning was available to each of us all the time, every day?

What if you really could look up from whatever is troubling you in the moment, and find the lesson staring back at you? What if your everyday troubles, themselves, were your finest teachers?

Yet, those lessons don't always jump up and present themselves in clear and easy terms. Sometimes you have to work for them.

A friend was struggling with a relationship issue in her job as a first responder. It was a beautiful spring day as we walked and talked around Lake Merritt, but she was angry and fed up with her job.

I could hear that an old belief was keeping her stuck, that she couldn't own her feelings in the workplace. Somehow she thought she had to be a strong, capable, 'together' woman all the time, 24.7. When I asked her what she'd say if she could say anything to her crew, she was silent.

Somehow my friend believed that unlike the rest of us, first responders aren't allowed to have feelings, even when they're not in emergency mode. And yet, as we walked and talked, her emotions were right there.

"What do you need?" I finally asked her.

She paused for a moment and looked out at the lake. "I think I need to be vulnerable at work, and talk about what's bothering me."

Bingo.

When we allow them, our emotions can be arbiters of real change in our lives. It's really very simple, but oh how we try to avoid this truth. We don't want to feel our damn feelings—and yet, they are the most direct path to the wisdom inherent in each crisis.

This is not to say we have to lash out, pound our fist and raise our voice. We can practice our words ahead of time, and deliver 'right speech' as the Buddhists so beautifully put it.

We can also make requests instead of shrill demands…and we can keep on politely making them until our issue is resolved. (And okay, some firm persistence may need to be used occasionally, but only after all else fails.)

Note: I'm not just talking about anger here. Sometimes what another person needs to hear is that we are scared. Or sad. Or that we simply need a pat on the back and a little support.

Wherever you are today, and whatever is bothering you, allow yourself to surrender to your feelings. Even if they take you to uncomfortable places you'd rather not visit. Your emotions are happening for a reason. And they are simply God's way of taking you more deeply into life.

There is no good reason to resist, no matter what you were told about your feelings when you were young.

And, as ever, enjoy responsibly!

How to Be Alone, Even on Your Birthday

This week I celebrated my birthday, and it was actually one of my happiest ever. Why? Because perhaps for the first time in my life, I am truly able to celebrate me.

Without any big accomplishments. No 'extraordinary cause for celebration'. No bells and whistles.

On my birthday, I gave a party for moi. And yes, I was all alone. Remarkably, I also happened to be in Paris, and that was pretty darn cool, too.

In the past, I used to secretly wish someone would throw me a big surprise party. I imagined it would feel like the whole world was lining up to throw their arms around me in a humongous group hug.

Then there would be a mass exodus of all of my demons, and I would live happily ever after. And I would finally know I was truly and completely loved.

But that is when birthdays can be a con. Because it is only when we learn to light our own little candle, and put it on our own little cake, that we get to live happily ever after.

I suspect this was the very best birthday gift I could give myself. For no one is ever going to love me more than I love myself right now.

And here's the wildest part. It is only when we can sit alone in both happiness and pain, and allow ourselves to feel, own and accept our grief and our shortcomings that we can begin to feel, own and accept true love.

Ironic, right?

Then we don't need the big elaborate bash with roman candles and champagne fountains to feel appreciated. Nor do we need any other person to tell us how wonderful we are.

Instead, life becomes simple and simply perfect.

When I did this recently, a remarkable thing happened. My spirit went into lift off, and birthday tributes somehow came pouring in. I opened Facebook and discovered hundreds of people had crowded my page with their beautiful good wishes.

I was so not alone on my birthday, as it turned out—I had good company.

A few times surprise parties were thrown in my honor over the years, and there were 'It's Christmas!' feelings for sure. But then the abundant magic always wore off. Life as usual eventually emerged, and I found myself trudging along again, no different than the day before my birthday.

But this year is different. This time the song was a simple 'Happy Birthday' sung from the heart by the eight-year-old who lives inside of me. I call her Little Susie; she's funny, imaginative and wants nothing more than to love people and have fun.

We celebrated by doing one of Little Susie's favorite things: swimming at a sophisticated spa in the suburbs of Paris. (OK, Little Susie has grown up a titch.) Among other things it had a pool-sized jacuzzi with all sorts of bubbling stations. Lumbar chairs with jets that massage your lower back. Lounge pools with beds full of bubbles. There was even a lap lane in which you could swim against the current.

It was like a water park for adults with a lot of tension…and Little Susie and I were all over it.

Then we had a lovely, rainy evening doing what we love best: making a little dinner and writing. And okay, yes, I did stop by a patisserie and bought myself a fabulous tiny cake for one.

Of course, I don't plan to spend the rest of my life alone, but of one thing I am certain. There won't be room for another in my life until I become truly intimate with myself. Because what I crave more than anything at this point in my life is that deep connection.

As I unfold more and more, following my instincts and surrendering to who I truly am, those connections are appearing. This is what is possible for all of us.

By doing nothing more than telling the truth and becoming humble, we find friendships that truly feed our soul.

Each day our job is simply to get up and do God's work. That's all there is to it. Then the drama disappears, along with the overwork, the hand-wringing and the longing for the eternal missing piece.

For me each day shows up like a perfect, peaceful gift for which I am grateful. And woven through all of it is the joyful presence of Teal, ever by my side. This, to me, is intimacy. Pretty soon I will become open to another person appearing in my life, but in God's time of course—not mine.

It used to be that I couldn't wait to find the 'other' who would complete me. These days, the rules have been lifted and the chains have been thrown off, and I walk freely towards the sun—whole, complete and uplifted.

This is my privilege and my gift. It is yours, as well.

I invite you to come along, for this path is paved with magic.

How to Stop Trying to Get Meditation Right and Just Relax

I used to be a really busy meditator. You know the type.

I could barely sit still because I was so busy feeling my divine energy consume my body, moving me this way and that. Or I was constantly opening my eyes, focusing on this timer or that crystal to keep my meditation 'on track' and perfect. Or maybe I was working on memorizing some really long, complicated mantra while I meditated.

Who had time to just become empty and still?

I didn't. I was too busy getting my meditation 'right' to actually relax.

But that was before I discovered the true, messy imperfection of meditation. In its simplest state meditation isn't anything in particular, other than stilling the mind. And that's hard to do…hence the plethora of meditation tools, apps, props, supports, recordings, mantras, breathing practices and experts. All of which want us to get meditation 'right.'

But what if there was no right way to meditate?

Only now, nearly thirty-five years after I began meditating, do I appreciate the value of letting my mind roam as it must. When I notice it, I gently steer it back toward nothingness. That's all I need to do, it turns out. Just kindly return myself back toward nothing again…and again…and again…and again…

When I do this, and my timer rings at the end of fifteen minutes, I find myself calmer than I was before. I'm refreshed. Ready to move into my day. That's what meditation does for me, and its benefits are subtle and deep.

I notice, for instance, that I've lost my old love for drama. Over time, meditation makes the mind lose its tolerance for chaos and chaotic people. Likewise, you lose your interest in that which grates. Instead, you become remarkably kind to yourself.

Now, when I make a mistake, I find I no longer chide myself. Instead, I remind myself that life is just this really big experiment. If I get it wrong, that's okay. Maybe I'll get it right next time…or maybe I won't.

Bottom line: It doesn't matter.

Really.

That's the big thing I've gotten from meditation. As the hours slip by, day by day, and your tolerance for pure nothingness increases, you can't help but embrace the now.

For that's really all we have, isn't it? Just right here, right now, in all of its unvarnished glory.

Mind you, I'm anything but perfect on this count. I find myself planning and strategizing as if I could personally plot out every twist and turn in my future. But I can't. Wordlessly, meditation reminds me of this truth again and again, without even trying.

But then, sometimes, things happen. Unbidden, sudden insights can drop in when you're meditating, yet you can't go looking for them. Instead, your only job is to relax…and empty your mind… and let go.

In 2010, Teal wrote in her journal about her own meditation practice, and I think this passage sums up this phenomenon nicely. She wrote it while she was backpacking her way through the world, one day at a time. On this particular afternoon, she happened to be in Italy.

"On my way back, I saw this cemetery…It was white marble and really amazing…overlooking the sea, cliffs, mountains, and towns. So I chose to sit down there and meditate and I got: 'Go to Thailand, open your heart, open your soul and be.

The whole 'be' thing really made an impact on me. I realized in life I am never really there. I tend to be thinking about the future or past or something someone said instead of being in the moment, and taking it in for all its beauty.

After this meditation, I knew I had been transformed because I looked out over the ocean and mountain scene in front of me and I started to cry. I was really able to take it all in and I finally realized how blessed I am to be here, and how many beautiful things there are here."

When you can finally let go and embrace nothingness, it seems the entire world opens up to you. You can literally get outside your frantically busy brain for just one minute—or five minutes. And so you can breathe again, and 'be' as Teal liked to put it.

It's ironic, isn't it? Because the finding of serenity, of peace, of true freedom, comes not from getting or seizing anything.

True peace is found only by letting go.

What's on the Other Side of Letting Go? It's Flow, Baby!

Once you do the hard work of letting go, an interesting thing starts to happen. You find yourself with nothing much to worry about.

There is palpable peace there, if you allow it. All you have to do is tune into the small, quiet frequency that lies just below the hectic pace of everyday life. You know this place…it's just beyond the to-do lists, and multi-tasking and the worried sense that you're not doing enough.

It's that lovely, floaty place you arrive at when you've been meditating for a while. You're calm, clear headed and you have no particular place to get to in that moment.

Instead, you allow yourself, for once, to be in flow.

Now, flow is a very powerful state of Grace. Flow is what brings miracles to your door, unbidden. It's what allows you to walk down the street and bump into the very person you were just thinking about.

Flow is also the stuff your dreams are made of.

Once you make the break—whatever it may be—and let go of the all-wrong situation you've been anxiously clinging to, and the non-stop worry that accompanies it, space in your psyche opens up. Your soul relaxes. Your heart expands.

You may even feel like humming or skipping a little. (Go ahead…it's actually kind of fun.)

Once you find yourself in flow, each day can take on an organic design of its own, no matter what you are up to. So instead of sitting down to a rigid, even overwhelming list of to-do's, do something radical and throw them all out. Instead, just sit quietly for a moment and feel what your heart wants you to do next, and next, and next.

Then do it. And decide you're going to make it easy for yourself, and trust the process you are in. You may notice a certain ease or lightness, or a sudden, remarkable passage of time as you dig in productively.

Even if your beautifully in-flow work occasionally requires you to do something you'd rather not, like attend a tedious meeting, you can still be in flow. Just ask that glorious state of flow to accompany you to the meeting and inform your presence there. Let it move you to contribute in the most beneficial way you can.

Ideas may pop up out of nowhere, and agreements are simply easy to make. Flow is always marked by ease and a marked lack of 'doing.' Things just show up, again and again, and they are always in harmony with what you want and need.

However, be aware that the state of flow resists certain situations.

If you cling to a job that is one hundred percent wrong for you or a relationship that's a struggle, flow will disappear the moment you step through that door.

Flow also disappears when you watch it too closely, or cling to it too needily. You can't shut your eyes, cross your fingers and hope for flow with all your heart. Instead, you must invite it in gently, graciously and without attachment. And then go about your business until it arrives. Only then can it do its magic.

Flow sometimes takes its own sweet time about showing up, which is its privilege. It will come when it, and you, are both ready.

Most of all, the state of flow is marked by desire. Whatever you desire from moment to moment will guide you most effectively to the state of flow. You simply have to be quiet to know what that is…

then follow the directions that well up from your heart.

Try it right now. What is it that you desire most?

Perhaps it's a gluten-free chocolate fudge tart. Okay, why not? Go get one…and chances are while you're walking down to the corner to get your tart, you will see something that will inspire a great idea. Or maybe you'll have a chance encounter with someone you need to meet.

Or maybe you'll just have an utterly fantastic chocolate moment. Thus becoming prepared more completely for your next moment, and the next one after that.

I invite you to delve into flow and let the rapture of it sweep you away. You will not dissolve, and you will probably be surprised how much you'll actually accomplish.

This is what life looks like on the other side of all that clinging and grasping that makes us suffer. It's free, easy and remarkably simple. And yeah…it's bliss.

Why not give it a try?

Tapping into the Joy of Life

There is a week each year when I remember and grieve the loss of Teal. It coincides with the time of her collapse, and subsequent death six days later. And I find it essential to my well-being to acknowledge it.

This is one of the really interesting things about losing the people you love. You either run from that reality, and so close down an entire world of possibility for transformation. Or you take a deep breath, plunge in and embrace the sheer awfulness of it. You stop everything and allow that grief to live in your heart for a while.

You cry when you need to cry. You lie on your bed and suck your thumb in fetal position, if you have to. You just allow yourself to fall apart completely. Then eventually, the storm moves on and you are left far emptier…and yet, far better for it.

For you no longer have to fight the demons in your own head that are trying to keep those feelings at bay. Turns out that's a fight you'll never win, which is why it's so much better to surrender.

So you surrender to circumstances that are bigger than you for a while. And you discover just how small and powerless you are in this grand life. In doing so, you rediscover yourself, your true self, waiting on the other side. That's when transformation happens.

As people sometimes say of these moments, you become better. Or you become bitter.

So my entire perspective about both life and death have shifted radically. I no longer face the world with my tough-girl game face of intimidation, nor do I need to lose myself in compulsive overwork, as I once did before her death. I've also lost the 'hungry ghost' feeling that I'm not enough, and so must push myself beyond all reason to achieve, achieve, achieve.

The other beautiful thing is that I stopped fearing other people, or what they may think of me. Instead, I've taken a major chill pill. Instead, I'm far more interested in having fun.

No longer must I know how everything will come out, or 'work hard' to micromanage and coerce results. Turns out I don't have to grip and hold on to be safe. What a great discovery this is, for it unpins you completely.

When the worst thing that can possibly happen comes to pass, you discover an unexpected sweetness on the other side of that crisis. A transformation comes that makes your entire life far better.

If you allow it.

Each day since Teal's death, I learn a little more about something she knew innately. She understood how to tap into the gorgeous flow that surrounds us, and ride the undulating waves of life with unexpected ease. She also knew how to accept what comes as necessary and important.

Teal was at peace with her epilepsy, the condition that ultimately may have killed her. (We will never know for sure, for her medically unexplainable cardiac arrest could have been caused by SUDEP—a rare and unprovable cause of death among epileptics.) Instead of fighting her condition, Teal worked with it, taking excellent care of herself and making her rest, her serenity and her health her top priority.

When she wasn't doing that, she was tapping into the joy of life. Because Teal also understood about balance.

After she'd gotten the needed rest, there she'd go. Heading off for a backpack adventure in Asia. Jumping out of an airplane in a tandem sky dive. Busking on the streets of Europe. Farming in France. Singing with her blues band in Austin, or teaching kids in Ghana.

That was all part of her plan, because Teal loved making friends all over the world.

She knew how to tap into the joy of life, as well. So I learn from Teal's example, and I do my best to surf life's contours every day. When I'm inspired to work, I work. When I'm not, I walk. Or I read. Or I daydream. And when life kicks my butt, and I get sidetracked into some drama or upset, I do my best to shake myself off, get back on the board and ride! It's a practice.

That's the other thing—I don't have to do it perfectly. My life, believe it or not, has become fun again. Even death isn't a particularly big deal any more.

Sometimes I feel Teal around me, speaking into that small, still space between sleep and waking. It's the very same space we heard a lecture about only a few hours before her collapse…the ethereal passageway that shamans travel in between the afterlife and our world. As the speaker explained that fantastical connection, Teal pivoted in her chair and looked at me wide-eyed, making sure I understood its significance.

I didn't at the time, of course. Because I had no idea she, herself, would soon be traveling those very airwaves.

One of the messages she gave me in this pre-dawn waking has stayed with me. It is this:

Do not judge death with the same limited mind that barely learns or understands the potential in life.

You feel that potential sometimes in life's magic—the touch of a lover's hand, the triumph of a long-cherished dream, or in the laughter of a child.

But you are afraid of that power and so you hang back.

Do not hang back. Instead, become quieter and quieter until you are fully suffused with the power and majesty of God who lives inside of you.

Then let go. Do what you want. Allow yourself to truly feel your own deep, soaring magnificence.

The full, God-given gift of life is available to those who do not fear death. For loss is only temporary, a fleeting stab of pain.

When I forget about this, and get lost in that sense of deep longing that comes with grief, I go back to these words.

How to Take a Day Off So It Really Counts

Recently, a friend complained to me. "I was going to play hooky yesterday and instead, I just wasted the day doing nothing. It wasn't very satisfying."

My friend, who is self-employed, did indeed stay home and rest. In my mind, at least, he appeared to have taken the day off. So what was I missing?

Instead, of doing something specific with his time off, my friend did what we all do. He web surfed, sat in a sunny window pondering life and ate snacks. Downtime actually happened—enough that his brain was indeed given a good rest.

What was missing was the *intention* behind his time off. He hadn't consciously given himself permission to relax all day. Instead, he stayed stuck in that slightly guilty, in-between place of wanting to take time off, and even needing to. Yet, somehow he couldn't make it happen.

My friend was unable to give himself a bona fide hooky day. Perhaps you relate.

There is nothing more restorative than giving yourself a day off, according to neuroscientist Dr. Tara Swart. She notes that in order to be fully productive, you need blood flowing freely through all parts of the brain. When you're stressed out or feel you've been treated unfairly, that blood flow doesn't circulate as well in the higher functioning regions of the brain.

"You're unlikely to collaborate or be really productive," she says. "It's better to take some time out or sort the problem out and then come back to work. You're more likely to think creatively and take a healthy amount of risk."

Indeed, Dr. Swart says that 'presenteeism'—people showing up for work even when they're sick or exhausted—costs corporations more than twice as much as absenteeism.

In other words, you actually *can* give yourself the day off, guilt-free. Perhaps even on a regular basis. It might even be better for your workplace if you did.

I once lived in a remote town of five hundred people, just south of the Canadian border. Getting to the nearest 'big' city, Burlington, Vermont, required an hour to an hour and a half of travel each way, depending on how solidly Lake Champlain was frozen. A ride on an ice-cutting ferry was often part of the equation.

It was in this isolation that I was living out my final days as a closeted lesbian married to a man. At this point, our children were in high school and college, and I was biding my time until it was clearly the right moment to leave.

Every day was an exercise in cognitive dissonance as I tried to square my 'straight' married lady persona with the lesbian I knew I was in my soul. In spite of the deep satisfaction of parenting our children, my life as a straight wife had begun to chafe.

By Friday every week, I simply had to flee. I used this weekly day off as a staple of my self-care, and the comfort it afforded me was amazing.

Since I was a freelance consultant, I kept my own hours. Every Friday morning without fail, I'd be on that 8AM ferry, heading toward the comforting routine of my weekly day off.

Stops included the café with the crackling fire where I hung out on social media and chatted with friends. Then I'd drop by the YMCA and swim, steam and soak for hours. Perhaps I'd get my hair cut, or go to Bikram yoga, or browse the library for a good book. Eventually I bought groceries and gas, and then I'd head home to my family just in time for the last ferry of the day. I always returned rested, renewed, and ready to be the van-driving soccer mom once more.

The fact that this 'hooky day' was chosen, planned and designed to be part of my schedule was what made it possible. I felt no guilt whatsoever about it. Indeed, it felt like survival to me.

Innately, I understood I needed this critical time off to make it through the paradox that my life had become. Today that reasoning still stands, even though my world has radically changed.

Now I'm in a happy lesbian marriage, and living in the Bay area. Days off don't happen as often, mainly because my life is in balance, and I no longer need that release. If anything, the opposite is true.

It's harder now to justify a day off because I am as content and fulfilled as I am. And yet...one could argue that intentional days off are *always* a good idea. For all of us.

The trick is giving ourselves the gift of that hooky day. Yet, just like my friend, I struggle with this. Can I truly justify the time away from my desk? Is it really true that blowing off a work day will ultimately help me get more done?

Here are three reassuring facts that help you make that decision for yourself. May you find them useful.

German researchers have found that disengaging from work by not being there makes us more resilient in the face of stress, and more productive and engaged when we are at work.

- The Project: Time Off study noted that those who took fewer than 10 of their vacation days per year had a 34.6% likelihood of receiving a raise or bonus... People who took more than 10 of their vacation days had a 65.4% chance of receiving a raise or bonus.

- A study in the *British Journal of Sports Medicine* attests to the power of green spaces. A walk in nature has been proven to lessen 'brain fatigue.' Even sitting and studying nature outside a window can have a similar, calming effect.

Wherever you're at with a hooky day, may I recommend you assess if it's needed…and if it is, then take the plunge. You'll return to work better for it, for sure.

The Value of a "Why Not?" List

One of the big illusions about life is that somewhere out there…it's better. Someone other than me is working harder, delighting more readers, and generally looking a lot hotter.

And so, presumably, they are on track to be the so-called winner. Maybe they even get to take home a big stuffed bear.

A part of our brain often gets fixated on how our lives should be…as opposed to how perfectly satisfying and wonderful they are right here and right now.

My friend Jon calls this sad habit 'shoulding on yourself.'

As in 'I should be working fifty-hour weeks building my empire,' or 'I should call my mother more often.' And let's not forget that perennial favorite, 'I should be ten pounds thinner.'

If you're like me, you slip into shoulding without even thinking about it. I notice I get particularly should-y when thinking about my work, no matter how much I've accomplished. And no matter what's going on in my life.

I'm thinking about my second wedding, not too long ago. These were the days of wine and roses! Yet my mind was squarely parked on how much work I could cram in before the guests start arriving… purely out of should-i-ness.

But was I actually getting it done? Not really. I was too distracted! I wanted to take a champagne bath, and try on my wedding ring fifteen more times. I wanted to call all the family and friends who were showing up for the big day.

I wanted to hold my love and look dreamily into her eyes.

Which I would have done…except for that taskmaster, Should, in my head. Silently, she tapped her stick against her hand and gave me the evil eye.

Here's the supreme irony of it all. We don't actually get that much done when we are being all 'shouldy.' We're much more likely to really rock the results when we let go completely and honor what's happening here and now.

Jon, who is a very wise soul, reminds me that even a state of inertia can be God's will for us.

Think about that. *Even a state of inertia can be God's will for us.* Wow.

After all, God's not standing around, worrying and impatiently waiting for results, right? We're the ones who do that.

Instead, God, or the Universe, or Spirit (or whomever you recognize that great guiding Force to be), invites us all to let go and slide into the great slipstream of love. And that's pretty much it.

Here we flow from one task to the next, effortlessly. Here we let go and surrender and find our way to whatever would feel right next.

So instead of a 'To-Do' list, may I humbly suggest a 'Why Not?' list.

As in…why not listen to your body, and simply do the next right thing?

Why not take a walk and watch the clouds for as long as you want? For if you do, some inspiration will surely descend.

Why not call someone you love and tell them so? Then your heart will expand just a little more greatly.

Or why not take a chance and submit a story to that hot media outlet you've been craving because suddenly it feels right?

That's flow, baby. I highly recommend inviting it into your life.

When we get ball-and-chained to our ever-expanding To-Do

lists, there is no room for us to breathe. So we forget the very core of our aliveness. This is how we get so very, very tired. We can't keep up, and the strategies we've invested our time, our money, and our belief in begin to crumble.

This is when the 'shoulds' begin in earnest. And rightly so, because (gasp!)…we might fall behind. And if we do, we know in our hearts we will never catch up.

This is how we wind up soundly parked in self-doubt. Which is exactly where I was when I spoke to my friend Jon. I needed to hear him say that there is no 'there' there. There really is nothing to push toward.

There is only the here and now, one beautiful day at a time.

May you join me in embracing what is, for all of its warts, bumps and obvious gaps. They, too, are God's will…just as you are.

You have been given a sacred job of simply being, my friend. So the question remains: Is that good enough for you?

So why not simply say 'Yes?'

How I Gave Up My Home and Found Freedom

I just moved again. Only this time, I've finally come home.

Since my one-time life fell apart in 2012, my undulating path has led me ever forward.

Again and again, I've been called to up-level who I am, what I do… and even where I live. Challenges have abounded. Wild waters have had to be crossed. Yet I have persisted. And now, finally, I am thriving.

Oddly, I followed the path that Teal, herself, followed in the year before she died. Here's how it went.

A few months prior to Teal's death I gave up my apartment in San Francisco and moved in with a lover. The relationship ended shortly after I arrived…and so I found myself without a home. A nester by nature, I always held having no home as certain death.

Being asked to leave or losing my home was literally my worst fear as a small child. Yet somehow, this time I rose above it and did something radical. I dumped my stuff in storage, packed a few lean bags and went off to find myself.

"Nice," said Teal approvingly. She, herself, had just landed in an apartment after six months of couch surfing with friends, preceded by six months of backpacking around the world. "I don't really need a home," she explained lightly.

At the time, I didn't get it. But now I do. Completely.

Home is our tether to who we are—which for me was a rigid,

inauthentic identity, forged in the crucible of a dysfunctional childhood. But now I was being called to let go of all of it and head for the unknown.

In fact, in my homeless state, I was searching for the supreme ideal that formed every moment of Teal's life: freedom. So it was that I wandered here and there.

I spent a memorable month sleeping under the stars at a hot springs filled with gentle, naked Californians. Then I traveled, visiting friends here and there around the US and Canada. I was back in California, subletting a home in a small women's commune in the wine country when Teal died.

With her death came a new level of surrender. Having a real home now suddenly seemed out of the question. I wanted nothing more than to drift, completely unencumbered by responsibilities. The last thing I wanted was to be alone in a house of my own.

I found my way to a small, safe cocoon—a sunny rented bedroom in Petaluma, a sweet little town north of San Francisco. My housemates were funny, interesting, and forgiving of my frequent need to disappear and sob.

My identity continued to disintegrate.

It began to dawn on me that I was no longer capable of doing the business coaching that had sustained me for the last decade. Really all I could do at this point was drink tea and write, with a long-haired cat tucked by my side. Then my aging, infirm mother died and so I received a modest inheritance.

This time I packed up and moved to Paris for two months—an act of self-liberation I know my mother would have approved of. Here I could let go of the last vestiges of the compressed, anxious high achiever I'd once been.

A room for a mere twenty euros a night landed in my lap. So I spent my days discovering the city I'd always idolized in my dreams. I walked through Paris every day for hours. I bought groceries among the well-dressed Parisians, made friends, and practiced my French with everyone who would let me. I peered in every fascinating, beautiful shop window I could find, and I learned how to use an unbelievably complicated French washing machine. I also ate my way from one arrondissement to the next.

I even pretended for a while that Paris was my home. It was very, very nurturing.

When I finally returned to California, I was relaxed, centered, and newly grounded. Just as Teal was when she returned from her own wandering travels in Europe and Asia. At this point, it was sixteen months after her death, and I found I was ready to emerge… somewhat. But only in the safest and tenderest of ways.

It was at this moment that a kind, loving old friend invited me to live with her for free, in exchange for some home cooking and a little pet care. Now I found myself in yet another new town—Sebastopol, known for its hippie bus mindset and chill vibe. Here I found my yogi, a kind and guided soul who introduced me to another of Teal's loves: goddess spirituality.

Every time I went to Kashi's studio and practiced the gentle, healing yoga she taught, I felt another part of my heart open and let go. It was here that I became fully, completely surrendered to the path God and the Universe had given me.

In Sebastopol, I set up the tiniest of roots. I rented a small office and created an altar, which I lit with electric candles and strewed with rose petals. Regularly, Teal and the goddesses would drop in and advise me.

For another sixteen months, I dissolved back to a new layer of calm, and simple Me-ness. I gave up trying to make money, and within a few months a paying gig writing novels came my way. Everything I needed simply kept showing up, again and again. I found that all I had to do was trust the path.

For real.

During this time, I stopped striving and as I did, the best thing of all happened: I fell in love. A hike with a group of lesbians led me to friends who knew a woman having a big party. The Girl Party, it was called. A gathering of the tribe.

I began that evening by listening to my body—an old Teal teaching I'd managed to learn—and going to a Korean spa near the party. I soaked in the near-empty pools, and as I did I felt Teal's shimmery energy envelop me. "What are you doing?" I silently asked.

"Preparing you," her ethereal voice whispered in my ear.

"For what?"

"You'll see…" The shimmer gave a little silvery laugh that whisked through me, then disappeared. So I soaked, and listened hard to myself, and let go and relaxed as completely as I could. Then when I was ready, and not a moment sooner, I walked down the street to the party.

I slipped in just as the doors were closing, and within moments I'd bee-lined my way to the back patio. Here a fascinating silver-haired woman began to talk to me in an oddly familiar voice. She smiled at me and I was smitten. We'd never seen each other before, but oh, we knew each other alright.

Now I live with my love, and slowly the foundation of our new life is being built. My storage unit is getting emptier and emptier as I let go of no-longer-needed pieces of my past. And each day we knit ourselves together on the soul path we agreed to an eternity ago.

In my new life, I am finally free. My self-imposed prison is gone. The need to suffer has lifted. The relentless perfectionist has been silenced, and the little girl who lives inside of me has been liberated.

I find myself now with a new and gleaming path ahead, not to mention a home. Every inch of it is informed by my three years of wandering and living like Teal did. In wonder, grace and curiosity, simply waiting to see what would happen next.

Seven Simple Ideas for a Happier Life

I woke up this morning with the most beautiful insight. I realized I genuinely love people. Like…everyone. It wasn't always thus.

This sense has been a lifetime in coming. Mainly because I spent a lot of my life mad at people. And who can blame me? I was Susie Codependent—forever controlling, cajoling, managing, and manipulating everyone in my path. I thought it was my job to force reality every step of the way…just to be on the safe side.

So when life didn't give me what I wanted, I was mad. That's what happens when we suffer childhood traumas. These can be anything from severe bullying to having an addict parent to an illness or death in the family. When this happens, we build ourselves tough little cages of steel to live in…and so we suffer.

Mind you, a lot of us were exceptional children. We were the kids who were wise beyond our years. We were sensitive, smart and we knew how to cope with any disaster. We were the responsible ones who stayed late helping the teacher after school—usually to avoid the chaos at home. And we were often the tender kids who couldn't play sports but wrote awesome poems.

Ironically, we were also usually the adult in the room—even when we were six or seven.

This becomes the gift of trauma and loss. We have heightened sensitivity, and an overdeveloped sense of responsibility. We have anger—yet we have empathy as well. We feel the pulse of life a little more deeply.

In adulthood, our work is to take down this jerry-rigged defense system we've build around us, and begin to build a truly intimate connection with the world. And sometimes it takes a real disaster to make that happen.

Losing Teal and my former life shifted my perspective immediately. Sure, I grieved, but I also relaxed, learned radical self-care, and turned the spotlight back on me.

The following ideas have become my guiding principles. They're simple, cost nothing, and don't require any 'doing.' (And no, you don't have to meditate, though that's always a help.)

1. **I don't need to make anyone happy but myself.** This has actually become my more important responsibility.
2. **I really can—and do—say 'No' whenever I need to now.** The sky doesn't fall. It's great!
3. **No one has to march to my tune but me.** Everyone else has a right to live their life *exactly* the way they want. As do I. If that means we need to go separate ways, so be it. It's always just part of God's plan.
4. **Things usually work out just fine.** Once you've been through the worst thing that can happen and you emerge better for it...you learn to go with what comes. Really, truly. Things do work out.
5. **Stop worrying.** Turns out worrying doesn't help—it just produces a lot of agita. So I try not to spend time there anymore.
6. **We can't force reality.** What a shocker! I seriously thought I could. Kind of hilarious when you think about it.
7. **In the end, all we've got is love.** Turns out accumulating stuff is highly overrated and somewhat lonely. But love really does heal all wounds.

May my little list help you in some way today ... or next year. Written with a hug ... and with you in mind.

How I Finally Learned to Open My Heart

Some years ago, a psychic in Key West, FL told me something I'm only just now beginning to understand.

As I sat there in front of her, in a darkened room heady with incense, she intoned: "You'll have the success you want, Suzanne… but only when you open your heart."

I wasn't sure what that meant, exactly, but I did what any good self-help devotee would do. I set out to crack the code on what 'opening your heart' meant.

My first stop was the aromatherapy store, where I spent a good hour sniffing this and that until I'd whipped up my own little brew designed to split open a congested heart chakra. (Mind you, I had no idea what I was doing, but this did seem like the place to start.)

Then I headed over to my friend, Mary, the Oriental Medicine Woman. Mary listened to me quite seriously when I requested she set lots of needles that would open my heart. After the third treatment, she gingerly asked how it was going.

"I don't know," I replied.

"Well, what would 'opening your heart' look like?" she asked.

Again, I could not answer. Meanwhile, a nightly application of my heart chakra oil was giving me nothing but a greasy, rose-scented chest. Ultimately, I forgot about opening my heart as the whirlwind of life sucked me on toward the next endeavor.

Then one night I sat up in bed, suddenly aware of exactly what opening my heart really meant. At the time, it meant working extremely hard on my passion, and investing time, money, and energy in getting it out there to share with the world. It also meant facing down fear, and being uncomfortable, and having the courage to truly share myself with others.

I thought I had learned this when I learned to lead workshops. During the weeks and months it took to create the first one, I was racked with doubt. I had to keep making one uncomfortable phone call after another. Yet, when that first workshop was over, we all seemed to be floating a few feet above the ground.

For the first time, I saw how I had the power to move people. The feeling was one of deep, intimate connection with others. It was profound and unforgettable. And I was hooked. This was exactly where I was meant to be.

Now, decades later, 'opening your heart' has come to mean something else, yet again.

In the first few years after losing Teal, it meant having the courage not to work incessantly, but instead to become very still and focus on feeling. To let my own grief well up inside until it found its way out into the broad daylight. And to let myself have the luxury of many a good, long cry.

It also meant allowing myself the 'work' of just resting.

Then, as my grief receded and I returned to the swing of life, I found opening my heart meant tuning in to the people around me. Now I learned to do my work simply for the sake of love.

In this way, I found my way back to empathy, and true forgiveness. This was a deep, deep place of surrender, humility and grace. Over the last few years I learned, for instance, to *really* forgive my suicidal, alcoholic mother. To finally let that poor woman, as flawed as she was, off the hook.

I have also learned to cut myself a break as well. No longer do

I have to do everything perfectly. Nor must I intimidate or impress people with my toughness, my brains, and my professional valor. Nor do I need to run from every person I fear or even disagree with.

Instead, these days I can be the softer, gentler Me. And I can listen to others. Turns out it's pretty damn fun.

After Teal's death, I began to make a conscious practice of sitting silently and listening when I met someone new. I would simply relax on the other side of the table, or wherever we were, and let the conversation unfold. I didn't strive. I didn't push. I just sat there and received the grace of meeting another soul.

I did this, in part, to honor Teal's memory, because she was always a generous listener who held no judgments, and instead waited to discover who people were. It was time for me to learn to do this, as well.

Once I finally slowed down enough to hear what others had to say, I discovered something striking. The rest of the world was fascinating. But you never learn this until you truly listen.

As I slowed down, I found I could also tune into my own needs. I found I could comfort myself—and hear myself—and even make requests to the outer world when needed.

In forgiving the world, I have learned to forgive myself, as well. And so I dissolve into love.

This is the love that waits, like a pool in our heart, for us to come swim in its bliss. And it is nothing more than our own shimmering, endless sea of bounty.

You have it and I have it.

Turns out *this* is the gold that awaits when we open our heart.

Go within to find your own place of letting go. What or who holds you fast in resentment, anger, chaos or confusion? What is the decision you made that you cannot forgive yourself for?

What is the loss you cannot face? What is the frightening choice that will set you free?

Perhaps not today, but soon you will find yourself releasing the bonds that hold you fast so you, too, may swim in the sea of bliss. The water's fine, my friend. I encourage you to dive right in.

A Lesson in Being from Teal

Teal was big on 'being.'

"Just be," she'd chide me again and again. I had no idea what this meant exactly, or so I told myself. Back then, I had no patience for Teal and her ethereal wisdoms. Instead, I was all business all the time.

A well-known Bay Area life coach shared a story at her memorial. She and Teal had lunch together, ostensibly so she could give Teal some much-needed career advice. Yet, in the end, she was the one who ended up unloading her burdened heart to Teal, finding herself in tears as she talked.

"It's simple," Teal told her. "Just be."

Well, okay. 'Just being' is not so easy for most of us—nor was it even for Teal in her lifetime. As a direct result of 'just being,' and moving through life and relying solely on her instincts and her spiritual guidance, she sometimes felt lost and afraid.

Obstacles would appear. The way would appear cloudy and uncertain. That's when she'd call me up in tears. 'Oh, Mom," she'd cry, and then she'd have a good five-minute sob. The exact cause was never clear, but it had to do with a longing to be like everyone else. She wanted to find her box that she fit into neatly, like the rest of the world.

Yet, there was no box that could contain a truly free soul like Teal. In the tattered red spiral notebook containing her deepest insights and revelations, she wrote this in her rounded, quick hand:

It is right for you to be you here because you are here.

As it turns out, these are words of wisdom for those of us who like to hold on tight for dear life, refusing to let go and look at the cost of our resistance.

Take this to heart. Wherever you are in this life, it truly is just where you are meant to be. Even if it's stinky, horrible, challenging and fraught with fear.

Even if you long with all your heart to be in some radically different place.

Even if everyone around you seems to have it ten times easier.

It is right for you to be here because you are here.

Listen to your heart, your body and your spiritual guidance. Trust that path. And know that whatever you are going through is temporary.

The experience of all that longing and pain will ultimately deliver you to that right place. Once you truly let go, follow your heart, and take the next right step, and the next and the next…then you will grow in wisdom, confidence and life learning.

You'll understand what Teal knew so well—that life, itself, is our finest teacher. But only if we let her in, embrace her, and honor her as the grand, beautiful, messy experiment that she is.

This, most certainly, is the path to joy.

All we have to do is 'just be.'

More on Self-Care from Suzanne

You'll find more of Suzanne's special brand of self-care in her free Self-Care Resource Library. It's yours in a click at: suzannefalter.com/freeresources.

Suzanne's healing podcast, **Self-Care for Extremely Busy Women,** helps you slow down and relax. You'll also hear from current experts about all kinds of self-care. You can find it on your smart phone's Podcast app, iTunes, Spotify and most podcast directories.

Suzanne's quick and easy online course, **Self-Care for Extremely Busy Women,** helps you focus on your own self-care and make a powerful plan in under two hours. Find it at suzannefalter.com/selfcare.

Suzanne would also love to have you in her **Self-Care Group for Extremely Busy Women on Facebook**. Just type Self-Care into Groups on Facebook and join us!

Finally, would you consider leaving a review of *The Joy of Letting Go* on Amazon? We would be highly grateful!

About the Author

Suzanne Falter is an author, speaker, blogger and podcaster who has published both fiction and non-fiction, as well as essays. She also speaks about self-care and the transformational healing of crisis, especially in her own life after the death of her daughter Teal. Her non-fiction books also include *How Much Joy Can You Stand?* and *Surrendering to Joy*. Suzanne is also the host of podcast Self-Care for Extremely Busy Women.

Suzanne's essays have appeared in *O Magazine*, *The New York Times*, *Elephant Journal*, *Tiny Buddha* and *Thrive Global* among others. Her fiction titles include the Oaktown Girls series of lesbian romances, and the romantic suspense series, Transformed. Her non-fiction work, blog, podcasts and her online course, Self-Care for Extremely Busy Women, can be found at www.suzannefalter.com and on Facebook, Twitter, Instagram, YouTube, and Pinterest.

She lives with her wife in the San Francisco Bay Area.

Acknowledgments

My gratitude goes to the wonderful team who helps me produce this work. Danielle Hartman Acee does a gorgeous job with proofreading and production of these books. Tim Barber of Dissect Design is our awesome cover artist. Tim Hallowell of The Podcasting Group edited and produced our audiobook edition. And my love, Rachel, helped me keep on going. Thank you all so much for giving this work your time and your talents!

More Books by Suzanne

Non-Fiction
The Extremely Busy Women's Guide to Self-Care
Surrendering to Joy
How Much Joy Can You Stand?

Fiction
Driven: An Oaktown Girls Novel
Committed: An Oaktown Girls Novel
Destined: An Oaktown Girls Novel

Transformed: San Francisco
Transformed: Paris
Transformed: POTUS
(All titles by Suzanne Falter & Jack Harvey)

www.ingramcontent.com/pod-product-compliance
Lightning Source LLC
Chambersburg PA
CBHW051345040426
42453CB00007B/427